Who Will Rise UP?

Jed Smock

HUNTINGTON HOUSE INC.

Shreveport • Lafayette
Louisiana

Copyright 1985 by Jed Smock
ISBN Number 0-910311-25-0
Library of Congress Catalog Number 84-0627777
Printed in the United States of America

DEDICATED
IN MEMORY OF MY FATHER
FOR HIS GODLY EXAMPLE
AND FAITHFUL SUPPORT

TABLE OF CONTENTS

INTRODUCTION

The mind-set of the typical college professor is to either ignore or ridicule and discredit the Christian faith. Searching for an excuse to rebel against God, I quickly fell for the lies of my University of Florida teachers. I swallowed the theory of evolution, gulped down secular humanism and slurped in socialism.

The students that I met who named the name of Christ hardened me in my unbelief. With their mouths they spoke of much faith but their lives said, "Jesus is not alive" and "No truth in Christianity." There was the "fundamentalist" freshman whom I met at a dorm beer bash. He spent the rest of the quarter taking me to movies, parties and yes, of course, trying to get me to pray the "sinner's prayer." I thought, "He is living the same kind of life that I am. What has Christ done for him?"

By my sophomore year I blatantly scoffed at God, denied Jesus and classified the Bible as man-made myth. In my utter ignorance and total depravity I smurked the familiar argument, "There is no PROOF." Even though I had blinded my own eyes to the obvious evidences, God in his mercy was pleased to show me even more truth. He did this through one determined soldier of the cross: JED SMOCK. "Brother Jed," as the students call him, preached holiness: total obedience to God from a right intention of heart. This was unusual enough but the convincing blow was that he really lived it.

When I realized this I asked, "How can a man be holy without the power of God?" Jed assured me that it was through Christ alone that he had been made free indeed from sin. Persuaded that Jesus is real I knew that the right and reasonable thing to do was to forsake sin and follow him.

I now know that I would be obligated to obey Christ even if every soul in the world were a hypocrite. However, I am proud to report that Jed has never let me down. I have known him for over seven years. We have been married since July 30, 1983 and I have never seen him commit one sin. The grace of God is powerful! Chapter 13 of I Corinthians, often called the "love chapter," is a perfect description of my husband. He truly loves, honors and cherishes me as he vowed to do. The Bible instructs wives to consider Sarah, who called Abraham "lord," as an example for us. And like her, I find great joy in serving and obeying my wonderful husband.

From the beginning I looked to Jed as a Knight in Shining Armor. The type of man that today's girl would never dream exists. He is strong, courageous, fearless, unshakable and best of all — HOLY. He is governed by disinterested love and a supreme desire to promote the Kingdom of God. He has the heart of an evangelist, the voice of a prophet and the commitment of a martyr. His heart thumps for revival and agonizes for a return to holiness and righteous living. No doubt he is an apple of God's eye.

Jed Smock has spent the last decade preaching on the university campuses of America. He may be the only preacher that is better known among the sinners than the saints. Five days a week, five hours a day, he can be found at an open-air rostrum confronting college students with the truths of God. Therefore the majority of collegiates have either heard or heard of him.

Christians have said that they cannot mention the name of Christ around campus without someone bringing up "Brother Jed."

Jed is very qualified to address the university community. He has been around academe most of his life. His late father was head of the English Department at Indiana State University. That is where Jed earned a B.S. in Social Studies, a M.S. in U.S. History and did postgraduate work in counseling and psychology. He taught for five years at the junior high, high school and college levels. It is no surprise that after his conversion, he would want to return to familiar stomping grounds and proclaim the great salvation of our Lord! In spite of insults, scorning and constant haranguing, he never grows weary of well-doing. In spite of being pied, egged, mobbed and even physically abused, his love for the students has never failed. Each day he joyfully enters the battlefield hoping to snatch more souls from the flames.

Many look at an outdoor preacher as someone who cannot get into the pulpit. Often, those who start with an open-air ministry let it fall to the wayside when they become popular in the churches. Jed refuses to let this happen. Even though he has been well received in congregations across the country, he always puts the campuses first. He has been faithful to leave the ninety-nine to find the one lost lamb. He often speaks for several hours each afternoon on campus and then holds nightly meetings in a local church. For this we can be grateful because the church as well as the secular world desperately need to hear Jed Smock's timely message.

Sister Cindy Smock

*If you can tell one person
about me you can preach. Just say
the same thing, but say it louder so
everyone can hear. — The Spirit of God.*

1

CRASHING
A ROCK CONCERT

Thousands of youth are gathering along the Wabash River for a rock 'n roll concert. Sunday morning church services are dismissing all over Terre Haute, Indiana. Even "Christian" youth are hurrying home to change into their cut-offs and T-shirts to rush to the annual festival in Fairbanks Park. Parents are blindly dropping off their children for an afternoon of "fun." Several streets over, Indiana State University students awake after a night of partying and are preparing eagerly for the day of revelry. Preachers and parishioners are going home to dinner and rest.

The stage is set for an all-day and into-the-night concert. Five thousand youth will soon congregate to worship at Satan's altar of sound and fleshly pleasures. Their rock priests are setting their instruments in place to lead the afternoon worship. The sacraments of marijuana, wine, LSD and cocaine are already being served.

A generation of youth is falling into the grip of Satan's fiends.

A generation is being lost to drugs, drunkenness and debauchery. Although the police station is just two blocks away, the lawless have nothing to fear. The Christian community seems oblivious to the blasphemous scene.

However, the eyes of the Lord are searching to and fro over the Wabash Valley looking for a man to stand in the gap. The Spirit of God is asking, "WHO WILL RISE UP FOR ME AGAINST THE EVIL DOERS? OR WHO WILL STAND UP FOR ME AGAINST THE WORKERS OF INIQUITY?" (Psalm 94:16).

Will anyone answer or even hear?

Church was running late that morning at Rosedale Assembly of God. I was kneeling at the altar seeking the will of the Lord. My soul was burdened for the thousands who were gathering for this diabolical event.

The Spirit of God spoke to me, "I will make a way for you to preach to 5,000 people today at that concert."

"But Lord," I replied, "I have never preached before." I had witnessed one-on-one and spoken to small groups, but I had not preached.

God answered, "If you can tell one person about me you can preach. Just say the same thing, but say it louder so everyone can hear."

I, too, attended the concert the year before with a wine bottle in one hand, a joint of marijuana in the other and my head filled with LSD — my hair flowing over my shoulders blending with a big, bushy beard. Half-naked, I danced myself into a frenzy. But a year had passed and I returned, saved and filled with the Holy Spirit, clean shaven, hair cut, wearing a coat and tie — fully clothed and in my right mind.

The concert's chief attraction was the Doobie Brothers. (They are not brothers, and their last name is not Doobie). A doobie is a joint of marijuana.

The Doobies finished their set with a song that was popular in the early 70s, "Jesus Is Just All Right With Me." The crowd danced wildly and sang along. There was an intermission when the group left the platform. This was my cue.

I jumped on to the stage, grabbed the microphone and proclaimed, "Jesus is just all right." Pointing toward heaven, I declared, "That means he is all righteousness."

The crowd objected, "What do you mean, man, we are the beautiful people?"

I preached my first salvation message to the stunned crowd for 10 minutes. God prevented security from interfering. When I leaped from the platform, a young man shook my hand and said, "While you were preaching, I surrendered my life to Jesus Christ."

At church that night I told the exciting story.

Prior to my conversion I had been the typical stereotyped, mealy-mouthed college professor. Most students would not have listened to me five minutes if they had not been required to attend class. Now I was a man with a message — a message of life and death. God had filled me with the Holy Spirit and empowered me to capture an audience and deliver a message that held people's attention.

This was the beginning of an open-air ministry that over the next decade would take me to 400 university campuses in every state except Alaska.

*By my 16th birthday I had
settled into a lifestyle of
drunkenness and dissipation.*

2

EARLY LIFE

I was born in Brookings, South Dakota, January 4, 1943. My mother wished to call me George Edward after my father. He, in an effort to avoid future confusion, suggested the nickname Ged — taking the G from George and Ed from Edward. I have always spelled it Jed. This is a biblical name meaning "beloved of the Lord."

My father held a Ph.D. in English from Cornell University and my mother an A.B. from Syracuse University. Father desired to marry mother when she graduated from college in 1932. But mother's father, a newspaper publisher and editor, had sacrificed to finance her education during the depression and he intended for her to teach the necessary three years to qualify for a permanent teaching certificate. This she felt obligated to do, so it was not until 1935 that my parents were married.

Mother never used that teaching certificate! She and my father spent the first 11 years of their life together in Brookings where he was chairman of the English Department at South Dakota State College. Father considered it his responsibility to provide for the family and mother wanted to care for her husband, three sons and daughter.

My father's interests and abilities were directed towards administration rather than the more scholarly pursuits of academic life. In 1946 he accepted the chairmanship of the Department of English at Indiana State Teacher's College in Terre Haute. Operating under the policy of only buying what he could pay for on a professor's salary, father provided a comfortable standard of living for his family. At an early age I learned a respect for books. To the chagrin of mother, father filled the house with them.

My father was active in the Methodist Church as usher, Sunday school teacher and board member. He led a moral and upright life, coming home to his family every night. He did not smoke or drink or use profanity.

Although mother was active in church work and community organizations, she made it a point to be home when her children returned from school. Having graduated valedictorian from high school and magna cum laude from college, her education was not wasted for she devoted a great deal of time to instructing her children and helping with their homework.

Like my mother, my father honored his parents. His father had been a prominent banker and county auditor in Delphi, Indiana, until his death in 1926. His mother lived to be 102 years old. When she became feeble, my parents brought her into our home and gave her the master bedroom where she lived the last 10 years of her life.

Grandmother Smock was a devout Baptist who loved to tell me Bible stories when I was a boy. She regularly exhorted me to moral behavior by reminding me that there was "good blood in my veins" and that I should never do anything to dishonor my family heritage.

The only "vice" my parents had was a monthly bridge party with three other couples on the faculty. Three times a year the couples met in our home for dinner and bridge, but the "party" was over by 11. None of them smoked and intoxicating beverages were never served in our home.

My parents faithfully took us to church and Sunday school as we were growing up. However, the insidious leaven of liberalism had been slowly creeping into the Methodist Church for years to the point the teaching was no longer Bible-centered. I ignored the little truth which was still taught by my teachers or the pastors. My Sunday school teacher, Mrs. V.L. Tatlock, however, gave me some memorable advice: "When faced with a decision, ask yourself what Jesus would do under the circumstances." Regrettably, I rarely hearkened to her good advice.

After feigning my way through catechism class, I was baptized and joined the church like the other twelve-year-olds. This did not change me or anyone else in the class. After refusing to make a heart commitment to God, I became less interested in religion as the years passed.

At age 14 I went on a weekend retreat with the high school Sunday school class. I refused to get out of bed for the morning devotions. Each night there was a time for discussion and one evening the minister brought up the subject of petting. Not having experienced intimate physical contact with girls, I was unsure of what he was talking about. The biblical standards of morality were not mentioned. This discussion sparked in me an immoral interest in girls.

My first experience in capitalism was in grade school. Fairbanks School was only one block from our house. Each day I rushed home, quickly set up a table and sold candy bars to my fellow pupils as they walked by. I bought the candy wholesale by the box and sold it for five cents a bar. In junior high school I had a paper route.

From grade school through high school my idols were baseball and basketball, especially baseball. From April through September I would faithfully listen to Bob Elsen broadcast the Chicago White Sox games over WCFL. Saturday afternoon I sat in front of the TV listening to Dizzy Dean relate the game of the week. It may have been during this time that the advertisement for Falstaff Beer implanted a taste for it in my subconcious mind. Sadly, the happiest event in my life during these years was in 1959 when Nellie Fox led the White Sox to the pennant. Mother used to get quite distraught with me because I referred to *The Sporting News* as my Bible.

My biggest disappointment was my failure to make the school baseball team. This was alleviated when the coach made me student manager. At Glenn High School the emphasis was on athletics, so if you were not associated with sports you weren't "with it." I did not want to be "out of it." What I did not know was what I needed was not IT but a person named JESUS CHRIST.

When I was 15 I began to recognize an emptiness in my life. Night after night I can remember lying in bed and thinking there must be some book to reveal what life is all about. Not once did I ever consider the BIBLE.

Although the Supreme Court decision of 1963 forbidding prayer and virtually outlawing Bible reading in public schools had not yet been passed, I never knew a teacher, administrator or student to suggest prayer or Bible reading in high school.

No one ever talked to me about a right relationship with God.

Drunkenness, Dissipation and Debauchery

My freshman year I began to run with a crowd of juniors and seniors. One night when we were cruising Wabash Avenue and I was sitting in the back seat of the car, a senior riding in front reached into his pocket. He took out a half-pint of J.W. Dant Whiskey and took a short swig.

Turning, he said to me, "Try a drink." This is the closest I had ever been to an alcoholic beverage. I did not even know what it smelled like. Without a moment's hesitation I took a drink. Struggling to hold it down, I passed the bottle to a junior sitting next to me. The bottle went around the car several times. Deceived into thinking this filled my emptiness, I began drinking every weekend. By my 16th birthday I was settled into a life-style of drunkenness and dissipation. Despite such revelry,

I graduated 11th in my class.

In 1960 I was a freshman at Indiana University. I joined the Delta Upsilon fraternity because they had the distinction of being the wildest "partiers" on campus. About half of the pledge class was already made up of heavy drinkers. My objective was to establish a reputation as being the biggest drunk in the class. By the end of orientation week, I had proven myself.

My sophomore year I purposed to out-drink the whole fraternity. By the end of the first semester I had accomplished my college goals. I did not know the biblical warning: "Woe to those who are heroes when it comes to drinking and boast about the liquor they can hold" (Isaiah 5:22 L.B.).

After a year and a half at Indiana University I dropped out and hitchhiked to California. In Long Beach I found a job selling encyclopedias door to door. One evening I made a two-hour sales presentation to a very attentive customer. However, I became very discouraged when at the end of my best pitch, the man informed me he liked the set very well but he could not read. That caused me to decide to give up my sales career and to resume college at Indiana State University. At Indiana State I mastered the art of cramming for examinations and carousing the rest of the time. I was able to maintain a good academic record and still party. The problem was that after the exam I could never remember the material. Nevertheless, I graduated with honors, majoring in social studies and minoring in English.

The only time I invoked the name of God was on Friday, "T.G.I.F., Thank God its Friday. I can go out drinking and not have to get up on Saturday morning." During this time, in deference to my parents, I usually attended church with them. I never heard anything from the pulpit to convince me of my sins.

After the final exams in my senior year I went directly to the bar. Late in the evening two of my drinking buddies got into a fight outside the bar. Trying to play the role of peacemaker, I was punched in the mouth by a six-five, two hundred and fifty pounder, and slammed against a parked car. I woke up in the emergency room being stitched up in the face and back of the head. The next morning, looking in the mirror, I was shocked and unable to remember what had happened. I called a friend and we laughed together as he related the whole incident to me. I still bear the facial scar.

Had I been familiar with God's Word, I would have understood the following admonition:

> *Who hath woe? who hath sorrow? who hath contentions? who hath babbling? who hath wounds without cause? who hath redness of eyes? They that tarry long at the wine; they that go to seek mixed wine. Look not thou upon the wine when it is red, when it giveth its colour in the cup, when it moveth itself aright. At the last it biteth like a serpent, and stingeth like an adder. Thine eyes shall behold strange women, and thine heart shall utter perverse things. Yea, thou shalt be as he that lieth down in the midst of the sea, or as he that lieth upon the top of a mast (Proverbs 23:29-34).*

That night I was back in the bar and the following words described me perfectly: "They have stricken me, shalt thou say, and I was not sick; they have beaten me, and I felt it not: when shall I awake? I will seek it yet again" (Proverbs 23:35).

I led a double life throughout high school and college. My parents were shocked when upon my conversion I finally confessed to my shameful years of drunkenness. I was always careful to cover my sins. At home I tried to cooperate and be congenial. My mother to this day can't believe I was as bad as I have described. She always said, "Jed was a good boy."

Truthfully, my righteous acts were as "filthy rags" in the eyes of a holy God. He knew I had never done one good thing in my life because I had always been selfishly motivated.

In 1965 I secured a position teaching United States History at Highland High School in Highland, Indiana. Although there were a few dedicated teachers on the faculty, many of them were moderate to heavy drinkers. By moderate I mean that they only got drunk on weekends. I administered so little discipline in my classroom that it is a disgrace to the educational system they hired me again the next year. During those two years I completed my master's degree in United States History at Indiana State.

Bored with the night life in Northern Indiana, I decided to take the advice of the 19th century journalist Horace Greely, "Go West, young man, go West." I had the illusion of many Americans that if I changed location my life would be better. The problem with that philosophy is that wherever you go you take yourself along.

I turned myself to wisdom, madness,
and folly — Ecclesiastes 2:12

3

THE MAKING AND BREAKING OF A HIPPIE

During the late 1960s thousands of wayward youth journeyed from all over America to meet the devil at the intersection of Haight and Ashbury streets in San Francisco. A popular hit song beckoned them, "There's a whole generation, with a new explanation, people in motion." But, alas, the explanation was as old as Adam: "As it is written, there is none righteous, no, not one. There is none that understandeth, there is none that seeketh after God. They are all gone out of the way" (Romans 3:10-12).

They came to California as self-righteous "flower children" claiming a new awareness and talking and singing about love; but inside they were full of cursing and bitterness. Captivated by a spirit which led them to rebel against God and his standards of home, cleanliness, purity and order they lived in the streets or "crash pads." Hair grew long, jeans became the dress code, drugs were the prescription and the message was in the music: "turn on, tune in, and drop out." "Destruction and misery were in their ways," (Romans 3:16) as thousands became addicted to drugs, conceived illegitimate children, aborted babies, caught hepatitis and became possessed with evil spirits.

Turning on, Tuning in and Dropping Out

In the summer of 1967 as I drove my new Ford Mustang across the wide Golden Gate Bridge my thoughts were far from the hippie life. I looked forward to the lively night life, bars catering especially to single people, sailing trips, weekends on the beach and riding little cable cars. Renting a comfortable apartment close to the University of California in Berkeley, I found a job teaching junior high school social studies. It seemed that I was well on my way to following the career of my father. However, my life-style and future plans were shortly to change — radically.

One Sunday I decided to go to the Haight-Ashbury district to a rock concert where thousands of hippies had gathered for a "love-in." A man wearing a beard, long hair, cowboy boots, jeans and a leather jacket crept up to me and said, "Hey, man. I have something you ought to try. It will expand your mind. You will begin to see things that you have never seen before, and hear things you have never heard before. Here, try some marijuana." Attracted by the smell, I smoked the weed. There is a proverb that says "the eyes of man are never satisfied." I was not satisfied with a few "tokes" or a few "joints", but he very next weekend I was back at the Haight to "score my own lid."

Eventually, no longer content with marijuana, I journeyed on LSD trips and was emotionally carried about by the waves of electronic music as the rock superstars turned me into a wandering star reaching into the blackness of darkness. The Beatles sang, "All you need is love," but all I found was lust, as carnal gratification became the driving force of my life. Ungodly hippies became my constant companions in unknowing captivity as I marched into the streets shouting for peace in Vietnam and freedom to control the universities. The scriptures rightly said: "But the way of peace have they not known" (Romans 3:17).

I turned on to drugs, tuned in to the hippie scene and quit my teaching position to drop out and join the "revolution."

Soon the devil began to break up his training ground at Haight-Ashbury and on the Berkeley University campus. He directed his children to go home and sow his seed of drugs, disbelief, discontent and disillusionment in the virgin soil of cities, towns and rurals areas outside of California. Thousands of hippies returned home, not with the repentant heart of the prodigal son, but to "hook" their younger brothers and sisters and old classmates who were still straight. I came back to Terre Haute, Indiana, wearing long hair and a beard, cowboy boots, jeans and a leather vest stuffed with marijuana. I crept up to old acquaintances, saying, "Hey, man, I have something you ought to try. It will expand your mind. You will begin to see and hear new sights and sounds." With lying words, I seduced many into the use of drugs.

Dropping In

Harking to the deceitful schemes of liberals to work within the system to bring about change, I put on a business suit and trimmed my beard and hair enough to be hired as a professor of United States history at the University of Wisconsin. I taught a communistic interpretation of the past and presented the lie of evolution as a fact.

In 1970, the year of the Kent State incident, the cry was, "Get your head together man, get your head together." I thought "Yes, I need to get my head together; I think I'll study psychology — the psychologists seem to have the answers." So I accepted a position at Indiana State University as research assistant for the Institute on Research into Human Behavior. I studied counseling and did research into drugs. I wrote a master's thesis on the personal effects of smoking seven straight joints of marijuana. I was even given a job counseling freshman students in the dormitories. Having eyes that could not cease from sin, I beguiled many unstable souls.

Out Again

Finally in 1971 I gave up on fitting into the system and returned to my Levis and long hair. My attitude, life-style and appearance had become of great concern to my parents but, since my heart had become so hardened by sin, I did not care. To me their ideas were old and belonged to the era of Victorianism. They had lived their life their way; I was going to live mine my way. Therefore, taking money which I had inherited, I gathered together a few things in a backpack, took my journey into a far country and there wasted my substance in riotous living.

Making my way to North Africa, I hitchhiked down the coast to southern Morocco and joined a band of hippies living on the beach. Within a year the Haight-Ashbury scene had become a world-wide movement as scores of thousands of American youth just like myself were roving the globe as gypsies.

Living at the beach commune, I thought, "Man, this is really it; this is where I can do my own thing — be natural" — that was my philosophy. My standard was; if it feels good, DO IT. I became so natural that I started worshipping nature.

I would go down to the beach at sunset, get in lotus position and chant: "Ommmm, Oooommmm" This was supposed to give me peace of mind and make me more sensitive and aware of my "oneness with the cosmos;" but in reality it just opened my mind to the control of more demons.

These devils began to speak to me, "Man, you're always talking about other people's hangups; you still have a few of your own — you still wear clothes." Before long I was running those beaches stark naked. This did not bring me peace of mind, either.

"How much more natural can I become?" I thought. "I've been a good hippie."

Back home I had almost every Beatles' album. I had been to rock concerts and demonstrations all over the world. My hair was long and a beard covered my face. I had worn my faded Levis until the patches had holes in them. I had carried my army surplus backpack for so long that even without wearing it I naturally walked like hippies walk: shoulders slumped, back bent and arms swinging in an ape-like fashion.

I had turned myself to behold "wisdom, madness, and folly" by reading *I Ching;* the Herman Hess novels, *Siddhartha, The Glass Bead Game, Steppenwolf, Demian*; Allan Watts, *The Wisdom of Insecurity;* Ramm Dass, *Be Here Now;* and Thoreau, *Walden Pond.* Still, I had no peace of mind. Having cast off restraints of parental influence, job responsibilities, material possessions, financial burdens and church teachings, I was more bound than ever.

My madness and folly was communicated in a letter written to my parents from Morocco: "Despite passing my twenty-ninth birthday, I still feel young — but hardly carefree — a state of mind I would like to reach; but I still find myself projecting into the future or regressing into the past, thus making it difficult to trip on my trip."

Turning on the Light

"The way of the transgressor is hard" (Proverbs 13:15) — but God is rich in mercy! On Christmas day our hippie band had a beach party with excess of wine, drugs, revellings and abominable idolatries. Suddenly, an Arab marched into the midst of the party, planted a rugged cross in the sand and preached about Jesus.

Although most of the children of wrath mocked him, the Word pierced my heart and I began to consider how little I knew about Christianity. Despite having a master's degree in history, five years of teaching experience and studying extensively in the fields of social science, literature, psychology, philosophy, liberal theology — and even the occult — I knew almost nothing about Jesus Christ. I was headed to India to study under a guru. I was "Ever learning and never able to come to a knowledge of the truth" (II Timothy 3:7).

Remembering how mother had recommended the Bible, I wrote my parents and they mailed a pocket edition of the New Testament which the Gideons had given me in the fifth grade.

Starving for the Bread of Life, I began to devour the Word. One evening, after reading the Book of John, I went down by the ocean as usual to worship the sun as it set. But I soon forgot my chant and began to meditate on John 1:3, "All things were made by him, and without him was not anything made that was made."

Suddenly I saw a light above the brightness of the sun — I saw the Light that lighteth every man that comes into the world. Coming to myself, I arose and followed the light toward home.

During this time mother had never stopped praying for me and she had submitted her lost son to the "tender loving care" of the Lord. I returned to the United States in March of 1972 with the Word of God as a light unto my feet and a lamp unto my path. I read the Bible almost every day.

What Really Happened at the Burger King

In August of 1972 I was riding my bicycle through the parking lot of a shopping center in Terre Haute, Indiana when I heard my name called out with authority, "George, George Smock!"

Stopping my bicycle I recognized an old high school friend, Clyde Swalls. The brightness of his countenance startled me. God's Word says: "A man's wisdom maketh his face shine, and the boldness of his face shall be changed" (Ecclesiastes 8:1).

He had become a preacher and never had I heard anyone speak like this man. Surely he had to be sent from God for this was not the same person I had known 10 years earlier in high school. As he preached to the young crowd that gathered nightly in revelry, I was drawn to listen and my heart opened up to the truth. One night we went across the street to the Burger King, "Home of the Whopper!" Clyde opened the scriptures to me and I became convicted of my sins. That night in the Burger King, I found the King of Kings when I called upon the Lord Jesus Christ to save me.

My high school friend — turned preacher — then said that I should be baptized in water. Deciding that nothing prevented me from being baptized immediately, we drove into the country past the Assembly of God church where he was pastor. Beside an old covered bridge, about 2 a.m. Sunday morning, I was baptized. I came shooting up out of the creek with my hands lifted toward heaven, praising and glorifying God. In that moment, looking up into heaven I beheld his glory. Returning to the shore we noticed for the first time a group of campers lined up watching us. They thought: who are those men in the water fully clothed and shouting hallelujah in the middle of the night?

Holy Rollers

A few months later I was attending a youth rally at a Pentecostal church one block away from the house where I had lived in my boyhood. The church grounds had been a vacant lot when I was growing up and every summer a tent meeting revival was held there. The neighborhood boys would go each night to watch the "holy rollers." One morning a few of us arose early to search around the altar for coins, because one boy had found some money which supposedly had dropped from the pockets of the Christians while they were rolling, but we found nothing. Twenty years later after searching half-way around the world, I returned to this same location; and where the tent had once stood there was now a beautiful sanctuary.

After the ministry of the Word, the spirit of the Lord drew me to my knees at the altar and in the same spot where years before I had searched around for a few coins, God gave me something better than all the silver and all the gold in the world — the mighty baptism in the Holy Spirit. It was then that I was given power and a new boldness to be a witness into the uttermost part of the earth.

Hubert Lindsey saved the tax-
payers 10 million dollars in riot
control alone. — Ronald Reagan

4

"HOLY HUBERT" AND BROTHER MAX

During my hippie days in the San Francisco Bay Area, Jerry Rubin, Abbie Hoffman and Mario Savio rallied with other radicals to conduct massive teach-ins at the University of California at Berkeley. Like cattle going to the slaughter, hundreds gathered on the steps of Sproul Hall and were brainwashed with doctrines of socialism and anti-Americanism. The students were incited to massive demonstrations and rioting. Extensive media coverage of these events had lured me to the scene.

In the midst of this turbulence God had sent one lone, fearless, fiery-tongued evangelist — Hubert Lindsey — who answered the call to rise up against the evildoers. This one-man army invaded the radical territory — often crashing their demonstrations and drawing an even larger crowd to hear him preach. As a result, the lives of many police and students were spared. Governor Ronald Reagan said that Hubert Lindsey had saved the taxpayers of California 10 million dollars in riot control.

"Holy Hubert," as the students dubbed him, was regularly kicked, mocked and spat upon as he warned them to turn from their wicked ways and live. When the revolutionaries realized he was a serious hinderance to their movement, they beat him to the point of death over a dozen times. But his love for the lost never failed. He continued his battle on the Berkeley campus for more than eight years. When times were roughest on campus, Governor Reagan would call his staff to prayer for "Holy Hubert." The supplications of Christians in the Bay Area helped him endure until he saw many souls saved. Today some call "Holy Hubert" the father of the Jesus Movement of that era.

As a hippie I often saw "Holy Hubert" surrounded by a group of hostile radicals who were making comments and shooting questions with the rapidity of a machine gun. He always had an answer.

One day a long-haired student pushed his way from the outer perimeter of a large crowd and screamed at "Holy Hubert," "It takes an idiot to be a Christian. It takes an idiot to be a Christian!"

"You qualify! You qualify!" "Holy Hubert" responded.

Another student mocked, "Jesus saves! Jesus saves!"

"That's right, hippie, Jesus does save."

"He saves green stamps," shouted the student, and the crowd roared with laughter.

"Hold it little devil. You're right, Jesus does save green stamps and you're the greenest of them all. Bless your dirty heart."

A female Vietnam War protestor asked, "What about biological warfare, Hubert?"

"I want everyone on this campus to know I'm against biological warfare," he answered. "And as for you, young lady, you are an intellectual, spiritual and biological creature. I want you to stop your biological war against your Creator."

"Holy Hubert's" witty replies had the effect of silencing the hecklers and calming the crowd so God's message could go forth.

I stood on the outskirts listening attentively but did not mock or even ask any questions. The preacher's knowledge of the scriptures and his control of the belligerent crowd was impressive. I never imagined that, after my conversion, five years later I'd be doing the same thing.

"Holy Hubert" is now blind — partly as a result of the beatings he received at Berkeley — but he is still active in the ministry. Occasionally we preach together on the campuses.

Enemies Become Allies

Immediately after choosing to follow Jesus Christ I began witnessing to students at Indiana State University. This was a shock to many because I had been one of the original Terre Haute hippies. I was known for wearing long hair, a beard and ragged Levis before it was popular in the Midwest. Word of my new life in Christ quickly spread around campus. It reached Max Lynch, a Christian mathematics professor, who taught at the I.S.U. laboratory school.

Max Lynch had a reputation of his own. I had always considered him a right-wing religious fanatic. He was a man who stood up for God and country. Almost all other outspoken professors were liberal humanists who were critical of the American way, especially involvement in the Vietnam War. Yet here was a professor who publicly supported United States military intervention in Vietnam.

When I became a Christian my attitude toward Brother Max turned from that of ridicule and scorn to one of awe and respect. God ordained that our paths cross and two former enemies became friends and fellow warriors for the Kingdom. Frequently we visited and, sharing a common burden for the campus, we prayed for the lost souls.

Max Lynch had been a successful engineer for General Electric. In the spring of 1961 he suddenly realized that he had never sought the perfect will of God for his life. As a step of consecration Brother Max fell to his knees and asked, "God, what can I do for you?"

"Go to Farmersburg, Indiana and join the Friendship Baptist Church," God answered.

In obedience, Brother Max quit his job and went with his wife and five children to live in Farmersburg. He was hired by Indiana State University as a mathematics professor, taking a big cut in pay. Two years later he was called to preach and became pastor of a Baptist church and continued teaching.

From 1961 to 1968 Brother Max had the freedom to read the Bible, pass out tracts and even preach from time to time; but the radical elements began to grow in strength, and in 1968 the University president ordered him to stop these practices. This action provoked Brother Max to research exactly what his legal religious rights were inside the public classroom. He discovered that in 1963 the United States Supreme Court had outlawed prayer and virtually outlawed Bible reading in the public schools. Realizing the freedoms we had lost, Brother Max was shocked and enraged.

In defiance of the state, in the spring of 1970 he started opening his classes with a short Bible reading. The next fall the president gave Brother Max the choice of either discontinuing his Bible reading or taking an administrative position. Because he felt it important to keep some contact with the students in order to be a witness to them, he chose to stay in the classroom and to curtail the scripture reading.

Three years later God awakened Brother Max from a sound sleep and dictated a letter for the president. In the letter Brother Max informed the president that he must obey God rather than men and if God instructed him to read the Bible to his students he would. Shortly thereafter, upon God's orders, Brother Max resumed his two-minute Bible reading at the beginnings of class. This action caused an immediate stir on campus. Considerable pressure was put on Brother Max to recant, but he stood firm. Eventually he was given an ultimatium: the Bible or your job.

One morning he called me, and said, "Brother Jed, a revival is about to break out in my 10 o'clock class. I want you to come in and preach to them." He indicated that he expected to be dismissed at any moment.

I rushed to the class, shared how Jesus had transformed my life and called the students to repentance. Brother Max gave the ones who did not want to hear the opportunity to go to the library. Instead, a few complained to the administration. The dean of education ordered Brother Max to ask me to leave the classroom. I quickly made a closing remark and left, but the class period was almost over so we had succeeded in getting the Word to the students. I had the distinction of becoming the first guest speaker forced to discontinue his message in the history of the university. Yet several radical communists had spoken without interruption.

Brother Max was suspended from the classroom the next day and a few months later he was fired. Actually, this was God's way of promoting him to a higher calling — preaching at the nation's universities.

Ironically, the twin daughters of one of the humanistic professors who had complained to the administration later were converted. Brother Lynch's stand for truth had made quite an impression on them. Later, when they attended Indiana University, the girls regularly listened to Max preach.

For the first year after my conversion I had been ministering regularly in churches and to other Christian groups. I occasionally held outdoor meetings at Indiana University and Indiana State. I saw that I could reach more lost people in one day on campus than in weeks in the churches. God directed me to make the universities the main thrust of my ministry. Since Brother Max was now free, we joined forces and began touring campuses throughout the Midwest and Northeast.

The chief influence for my campus ministry was "Holy Hubert." Max Lynch was also a great encouragement. His maturity in the faith and knowledge of the Word helped me field the more difficult questions of the students. Paul's ministry at Athens was the primary biblical example for the campus ministry.

Rev. Smock, we're here to
guard you today as you preach.
— Lt. Thomas Godbehere

5

CAUSING NO SMALL STIR

It seemed like a routine day at Arizona State University in Tempe.

Many students had spent their mornings in classes — English, humanities, math, physics, biology, psychology, sociology, political science, economics. Some were heading for the student union to have lunch with friends. The more studious had secured an afternoon spot in the library for homework.

A library window gave a view of various booths set up on the front walk by campus organizations. Students at the stands were offering information about different groups, issues and causes: pro-choice, pro-life, young republicans, young democrats, no-nukes, U.S. out of El Salvador, communists, socialists, homosexuals, fraternities, sororities, Moslems, Christians and Jews. But, the average student showed little interest in these. Behind the booths, Cady Mall was filled with sunbathers and a few frisbee throwers. Their thoughts were on the temporal:

"Will he ask me out for Friday night?"

"Does he really love me?"

"I wonder if that blue dress looks good on me? I better buy some eyeshadow to match it."

"I'll cram tonight for that humanities exam."

"I hope we win the game."

"Tomorrow night I'll get wasted at that keg party."

"I wonder if she'll go all the way?"

"I'm tired of school. I need a break."

No one suspected there was an unexpected visitor on campus. No one would have believed that within a couple of hours the whole campus would be buzzing with talk of "religion." The students were unaware that the benevolent God of the universe was about to take extreme measures to provoke them into considering their ways. The fourth-hour class ended and thousands of students flooded the Cady Mall walkways.

I took my position — Bible clutched in right hand, left hand raised and aimed, and fired away. "HEARKEN UNTO THE WORD OF GOD . . ."

A large crowd surrounded me as I continued the message. "You homosexuals call yourself gay, but I have never met a happy queer in my life. You are not gay; you are miserable. Nor are you liberated; you are enslaved. You are enslaved to your lust. But God will set you free from your abominable sin, if you will repent and believe in his name."

As soon as I got those words out of my mouth, a lesbian shot out of the crowd and hit me in the jaw. She knocked me off the bench on which I was speaking. Staggering, I returned to my platform and resumed my message. The crowd restrained the deviate but suddenly she broke away and tried to tear my clothes. Why this lesbian wanted to tear off my clothes, is hard to figure out!

The police were already on the scene wearing their riot helmets. When the sodomite attacked the second time, they quickly moved through the crowd to me. They escorted me to a squad car and drove me back to my motel for my own safety.

The next day the incident got front page coverage in the papers. When I arrived on campus, six policemen met me. Lt. Thomas Godbehere informed me, "Rev. Smock, we are here to guard you as you speak today."

I took my pulpit in the center of the mall with the six policeman encircling me. One of the largest crowds of my ministry gathered that afternoon but the presence of the police subdued them considerably. At the end of the day the administrator in charge of scheduling campus facilities told me, "This is the biggest things we have had on this campus since the student demonstrations of the sixties."

When Paul and his companions came to Thessalonica, the city was set in an uproar. The unbelieving Jews cried, "These that have turned the world upside down are come hither also" (Acts 17:6). A few Christians can stir and shake whole cities, states, nations, yea, the world.

When the council of elders, chief priests, and scribes accused Jesus before Pilate they said, "He stirreth up the people, teaching throughout all Jewry, beginning from Galilee to this place" (Luke 23:5). He stirreth up the people. Oh! That his followers might be similarly inclined today. But alas, contemporary Christianity desires to soothe, placate, appease, pacify, and compromise with the world and the forces of evil.

After I have completed a campaign on campus, the majority of students know Jed Smock professes to be a Christian. They may not approve of my manner or message. However, I am confident that they have been confronted with the truth. Yet, there are Christian students and faculty who have been on campus for years and relatively few people are aware that they profess the faith. This ought not to be so.

The Destroyer

A campus minister approached me at the end of a day's preaching at St. Cloud State University in Minnesota and said, "Mr. Smock, in one day you have destroyed everything the Christian community has worked for in the last year. There has been a movement to expel Christian organizations from campus. We adopted a policy of peaceful co-existance with our opposition."

"Sir," I answered, "you are the problem. Jesus said, 'Think not that I come to send peace on earth: I came not to send peace, but a sword' (Matthew 10:34). You must wake up to the fact that we are engaged in spiritual warfare. Be a soldier, take the offensive. Destroy the works of the devil. Quit being such a pansy."

Often students ask, "Who are you people? What's the name of your group?"

"We call ourselves the Destroyers."

"The Destroyers? What kind of a name is that for a Christian group?"

"It comes from I John 3:8: 'For this purpose was the Son of God manifested, that he might destroy the works of the devil;' and from I Corinthians 1:19: 'For it is written, I will destroy the wisdom of the wise and bring to nothing the understanding of the prudent.' What better place to destroy the wisdom of the wise than on our state universities? Hence, The Destroyers!"

God told Jeremiah that his first job would be to root out, pull down, destroy and to throw down — then to build and plant. Since my initial 1977 attack on the Arizona State University campus, I have seen an annual improvement. The hecklers are fewer, the students are more attentive and the Christians are more supportive. The extensive police protection is no longer necessary. Twice I was invited to address the largest class on campus — the Human Sexuality class. The once-leftest newspaper was taken over by conservative editors. The early editorial staff had scornfully called me "Heaven's Hamburger," but one of the later editors praised my ministry for promoting a stronger Christian influence on campus. The following article appeared in the *ASU State Press* after we spent a week there in 1984:

"An Afternoon On The Mall With Jed And Cindy"

"The late afternoon shadows stretched slowly across the lawn in front of Hayden Library. The six o'clock hour was drawing near, the chill of evening was settling in, and in the waning hour of daylight, Brother Jed Smock was still preaching.

"The day of evangelizing had begun at 11 Thursday morning and except for a brief respite when Sister Cindy stepped in, Jed had been holding forth all day.

"Earlier in the week, the word began spreading around campus. 'Jed's back.' For those who had spent springtime at ASU, there was no need to explain who this Jed was. We all knew who had returned. For those who hadn't, it was only a matter of time.

"This year's visit brought with it a couple of changes — Brother Jed and Sister Cindy are now carrying on the crusade together as man and wife. Over the course of a day, they took turns speaking outside the library, ringed by curious, sometimes hostile, and always animated circle of onlookers.

"Their approach is at times a bit jarring. But then, it is meant to be. Most college students don't spend much time thinking about anything of true importance — especially the way they're living their lives.

"At one point Thursday, Brother Jed pointed out that most college students run around utterly confused about their sexuality. He observed that college men spend most of their time in a sensual frenzy trying to add another notch to their bedposts or wondering about whether or not they should eat quiche — the latest measure of what a 'real man' should be. College women spend most of their time fretting over expressing their 'sexual independence.' It's no wonder that they never develop the moral foundation necessary to address their sexuality in a mature fashion.

The more vocal members of the audience are living examples

of the confusion bred by the moral vacuity of our modern 'lifestyles.' The comments they threw back — most of which are unfit to print here — only illustrate Jed's point. If these people are so comfortable with the way they live, you wonder why they feel the need to defend themselves so vigorously. No one forces them to stay and listen.

"Cindy and Jed are not the first preachers to come to the University. A student in the audience told me that a man named 'Holy Hubert' used to come to campus. Although I had never heard of Brother Jed's predecessor, the student could recall to the last detail listening to 'Holy Hubert' preaching on the day President Reagan was shot. A student broke through the circle of students who surrounded him and announced news of the shooting. The audience became still while 'Holy Hubert' led them in a prayer for the wounded president.

"I later learned why 'Holy Hubert' no longer makes the preaching swing through college campuses. It seems he had been hit so many times in the face by frustrated spectators, he developed glaucoma and lost his eyesight. I couldn't help but think of 'Holy Hubert' when I heard members of the audience screaming about Brother Jed's 'intolerance.'

"There is definitely a message behind the seeming madness of their oratory.

"At one point Thursday, Sister Cindy told a story about a student who lived only to satisy his own insatiable appetite for pleasure. 'He really thought he was living it up. Parties. Parties. Parties. But one day he realized he had a giant void in his life.' For a brief moment the hecklers were silent. They heard in that parable a description of their own lives and felt the same emptiness.

"Watching the sideshow outside the library over the course of the week, I saw the same faces keep popping up in the crowd.

"One tormented young man heckled Jed on and off for 45 or so minutes Wednesday. Finally pushed to his breaking point, he flew into a mad rage and charged up to the preacher. He spewed incoherently for a couple moments, then stomped away in utter confusion and frustration. A few minutes later, as I was walking down the mall, I saw him standing outside the Social Sciences Building with a few others, proudly relating his brief moment at center stage. Thursday afternoon, there he was again in the front row of the audience.

"But he wasn't the only one who kept coming back for more. Another very vocal young man found a forum for airing his own inner turmoil. He was one of the last to leave Wednesday evening, spent most of Thursday in the front row and was one of the last to leave again that night. Like the others, no matter how angry he became, something in Brother Jed's words drew him back.

"By early evening, the complexion of the audience had subtly changed. It had thinned substantially and the atmosphere of unbridled hostility Thursday afternoon had been softened by a genuine sense of curiosity. Watching as that small circle of students dispersed, I wondered whether that curiosity would remain after Brother Jed has left." By: Tracy Fletcher

Personal testimonies prove that we have been able to help build and plant the Kingdom of God at ASU. After one of my recent crusades, I was mailed this thank you note: (It is a striking contrast from the lesbian's fist that greeted me on my first visit).
"Brother Jed,"

"I wanted to write and thank you for what you have done for me, and also to encourage you to keep up the good work.

"Recently, you visited my campus. Arizona State University. I went to listen to pass time — just like many other students. I had always believed in God, but never felt I could rid myself of my selfishness, and live a Christian life — nor did I really want to.

"I had heard you in passing talking quietly with your associate, Bro Cope. You weren't talking about the Lord, but about the attitudes of the students on our campus. Initially, I hadn't much respect for the way you were preaching to the students, and thought you were another rambling Jesus freak. I realized that you preach that way (after hearing you talk quietly with Bro Cope) to draw a crowd; and therefore, spread the Word of God. It was then that I was ready to focus on what you were saying not how you were saying it. It wasn't long after you left that I accepted the Lord as my Saviour. You are truly a part of my testimony!

"I thank the Lord, and I thank you Brother Jed! I know you will continue to lead others to Him."

In Christ
Marianne

Marianne boldly related her testimony to a crowd of students in our 1984 meeting at ASU. The next day more joy flooded our souls as Christians joined with us at the end of a five-hour meeting in a closing prayer for revival and the singing of "Amazing Grace." At least one convicted student concluded "how sweet the sound." He publicly decided to repent and follow Jesus.

6

THE MULTITUDES GATHER

Athens was the intellectual and cultural center of the ancient world. The forum at Mars Hill was the university campus of Paul's day. It could be called the University of Athens. For those interested in reaching college students it is profitable to study Paul's approach, message and technique in ministering to the ancient philosophers.

When Paul arrived in Athens, "his spirit was stirred in him when he saw the city wholly given to idolatry." Paul must have heard the voice of the Holy Spirit ask, "WHO WILL RISE UP FOR ME AGAINST THE EVILDOERS? OR WHO WILL STAND UP FOR ME AGAINST THE WORKERS OF INIQUITY?" (Psalm 94:16).

Paul volunteered. He disputed daily with people in the marketplace and synagogue:

Then certain philosophers of the Epicureans, and of the Stoics encountered him. And some said, 'What will this babbler say?' others said, 'He seemeth to be a setter forth of strange gods,' because he preached unto them Jesus and the resurrection. And they took him and brought him to Mars Hill, saying, 'May we know this new doctrine whereof thou speakest?'

Then Paul stood in the midst of Mars Hill and said, 'Ye men of Athens, I perceive that in all things you are too superstitious. For as I passed by and beheld your devotions I found an altar with this inscription, TO THE UNKNOWN GOD, Whom therefore you ignorantly worship, Him, declare I unto you!" (Acts 17:18-23).

Then Paul began to preach. What did he preach? He preached repentance, "God now commandeth all men everywhere to repent." He preached judgment: "Because He hath appointed a day in the which he will judge the world in righteousness by that man whom he hath ordained; whereof He hath given assurance unto all men in that He hath raised Him from the dead!" When the philosophers heard of the resurrection of the dead, some mocked — some wanted to hear more on the matter — and a few believed.

Annually, God has sent me to Athens to preach — Athens, Ohio, that is. At Ohio University, as on so many campuses, you can see the influence of the Greeks in the architecture. In the classroom they still study and revere the ancient Greek philosophers — Socrates, Plato and Aristotle. Greek drama is read and presented by the theater departments. The democratic form of Greek government, considered to be the model for the American form of government, is examined in political science classes.

Each year I stand in front of tall Corinthian columns on the campus forum and declare: "Ye men of Athens, I perceive that in all things you are too superstitious. You are so superstitious you believe something as stupid as that, or else you are overly schooled. You're not educated because an educated man would not believe such a ridiculous lie as evolution."

Capturing Their Attention

People often ask: How do you draw a crowd on these campuses?

The Bible teaches, "Wisdom crieth without, she uttereth her voice in the streets: she crieth in the chief place of concourse" (Proverbs 1:20, 21).

My first objective when arriving on a campus is to find the chief place of concourse. Typically, it will be in front of the student union where each hour students are rushing to and fro from classes seeking knowledge. God commanded Isaiah, "Cry aloud, spare not, lift up thy voice like a trumpet and show my people their transgression, and their sins" (Isaiah 58:1).

With the voice of a trumpet blast I proclaim my favorite text for campuses, I Corinthians 6:9, "Hearken unto the Word of God, know ye not that the unrighteous shall not inherit the Kingdom of God?"

"Be not deceived; neither fornicators nor adulterers shall inherit the Kingdom of God. And it is commonly reported there are whores and whoremongers on this campus."

"Be not deceived; drunkards shall not inherit the Kingdom of God. And it is commonly reported there are drunkards on this campus — especially the fraternity boys."

"Be not deceived; idolaters shall not inherit the Kingdom of God. This would include all you rock 'n roll freaks."

"Be not deceived; neither the effeminate nor homosexual shall inherit the Kingdom of God. And I even understand there are sissies and queers on this campus."

This captures their attention! Within minutes several hundred students have gathered. Open air campus speakers are unusual. It is even more unusual for one to draw a crowd.

Students wonder:

"Is he for real?"

"Is this a production of the drama department?"

"This should not be allowed. Someone call security."

"Why, he is condemning us! Who is he to condemn us?"

"He's calling every girl on campus a whore!"

"He's crazy!"

"I've got to hear this! I'm going to cut class."

"My roommate should hear this!"

"I heard that he was at the University of Kentucky last week."

"This is great! I have never seen so many people listening to the Word of God!"

"Turn some water into wine for us."

"Crucify him!"

Paul acknowledged to the Greeks that "the preaching of the cross is to them that perish, foolishness; but unto us that are saved it is the power of God" (I Corinthians 1:18).

The Two Edged Sword

Many consider this approach "too strong," but "The Word of God is quick, and powerful, and sharper than any two edged sword" cutting swift and deep into our innermost thoughts and desires, exposing the sinner for what he truly is — totally depraved.

Too often preachers have spared God's Word. The sword of the Word has two edges. On one edge is God's grace, but on the other edge is God's law. On one edge is God's love, but on the other edge is God's wrath. On one edge is God's mercy and forgiveness, but on the other edge is his justice and judgment. His word says: "Behold therefore the goodness and severity of God" (Romans 11:22).

The point of the sword is holiness unto the Lord. He said: "Be ye holy for I am holy" (I Peter 1:16).

Regretably, today's evangelism has broken off the point of the sword and has filed down the edge that speaks of God's law, wrath, justice, judgement and severity. Consequently, today's Gospel lacks power and is without conviction.

Some say, "But I don't think you ought to call them queers." Well, you ought not to call them gay. God calls them abominable, they call themselves gay. When Christians use the term "gay," they have sided with the perverts against God. These Sodomites do not need our sympathy — they need the truth which will set them free!

Others will say, "But what about calling them whores and whoremongers? That is not nice!" No, it is not nice. Sin is mean and deadly. One day a girl who claimed to be a Christian admitted that she was having "relations" with her boyfriend.

"You're going to have to stop fornicating," I said.

"Oh, don't use that word," the girl protested, "that makes our relationship sound so ugly."

There is something ugly about that word fornication. The King James Version uses these convicting terms to lay bare their illicit sexual behavior. Students in human sexuality courses will discuss the merits and demerits of pre-maritial sexual relations, but the Bible calls it whoredoms. In class they discuss extra-marital relations or an open marriage, but the Bible calls it adultery.

The devil paints a pretty picture of sin but the Gospel preacher peels back the paint and shows the ugly reality of lawlessness.

Debate and Dialogue

Initially, students are amazed, stunned and overwhelmed. Many have never met a preacher who loved them enough to tell them the truth about themselves. After the crowd had heard me blast their idols of sex, booze, drugs and rock 'n roll for about 20 minutes, many began to make comments or ask questions in an attempt to excuse or cover their sins:

"Where do you get your money?"
"Who is sponsoring you?"
"What's wrong if I sleep with my boyfriend?"
"You are turning people off!"
"How do you know the Bible is the Word of God?"
"Judge not!"

"What's wrong with homosexual love," an effeminate boy asked?

"There's no such thing," I answered. "Homosexuals hate God, hate their parents and hate one another. If they had love in their hearts they would not commit such wicked acts." He stomped off mad, but later returned with several of his perverted "friends."

A girl shouted from the crowd, "How do you believe on abortion? How do you believe on abortion?"

"I'm glad your mother did not practice it," I replied. "I'm sorry to say that a lot of the girls on this campus are so low that they will use vacuum cleaners on their unborn babies."

"You're just a male chauvinist pig," another girl yelled.

"Do you know what I think you are?"

"What?"

"I think you're a tomboy."

The crowd roared and she flipped me an obscene gesture.

Her friend dashed in front of me. With her legs spread and hands on her tight Levis she taunted, "I guess you think I'm a tomboy, too."

"No, contentious woman, you look more like a cowboy."

After a few more rounds the girls left but later returned and listened for the rest of the day.

Holding Their Attention

Debate and dialogue are two of the many tactics we use to gain and hold the crowd's attention. We don't have a captive audience like professors or most preachers. As the prophets of old, we have an urgent message to deliver to a group of rebellious, uninterested students.

In an effort to awaken the wicked, God ordered his prophets to present strange object lessons. Isaiah preached naked for three years (Isaiah 20:1-6). God said it was to signify the judgment that Ethiopia and Egypt would receive if they did not repent. Ezekiel was constantly giving peculiar illustrations to warn the stiffnecked Hebrews of God's impending judgments on Jerusalem. These combined with his great oratorical skills drew sinners who came for mere entertainment (Exodus 33:30-33).

The Gospel armory is filled with weapons the average preacher rarely uses. On stage, where men undertake to represent a character or truth, they use all the arts and spare themselves not at all. Why should not a man go to greater lengths when dealing with the living realities of utmost importance? The wise use of humor, satire and scorn can turn an indifferent sinner into a serious seeker.

The barb of ridicule makes sin absurd and foolish as well as wicked. Elijah mocked the false prophets of Baal. My portrayal of the cigarette-sucking college psychologist who deceived a silly coed with moral relativism has become well known. We go to extremes to illustrate truth in a memorable fashion. Unusual voice techniques and elaborate gestures are especially helpful. For example, throughout the afternoon I will often refer to the eternal home of sinners:

"The everlasting LAKE OF FI-RRRRRE!"

I cry out with my jaw quivering rolling the r's.

After several FI-RRRRES, the whole crowd is chanting along. It's reported that within a few days of preaching, the students are shouting, "You'll burn forever in the LAKE OF FI–RRRRRRE," down their dorm halls. They consider it a big joke but as they mimic me the fact of this terrible torment is being impressed on their minds. As they are alone at night in bed the Holy Spirit will bring all things to their remembrance.

Daily, students ask for my imitation of Satan's minstrel Mick Jagger of the RRRRRRolling Stones. On one knee and microphone in hand, I ape him singing their hit "I Can't Get No Satisfaction." The students applaud with glee as I portray their rock idol.

Suddenly, I seriously ask, "Why did that song become so popular? Why does any song become popular? The answer is because it has a message people can relate to. Despite all your boozing, cruising, dancing, fornicating and drug highs, you are not satisfied."

"Why do people get drunk or stoned? Obviously, to alter the state of their consciousness. Why do they desire to change their state of mind? Because something is missing in their normal state. There is a void, an emptiness in their lives. Everytime they take a toke off a joint of marijuana or drink some Miller Low Life, they admit this — 'I can't get no satisfaction.' "

The students are listening quietly. The ground has been plowed to sow a Gospel truth.

"The Bible says be not drunk, but be filled with the Spirit. If you get filled with God's Spirit through faith in Jesus Christ, you will no longer desire alcoholic spirits, you will no longer want to get stoned. You will no longer want to fornicate. Your desire will be to please God and keep his commandments."

Some heads are hanging in shame.

"Jesus said, 'Blessed are they that hunger and thirst after righteousness; they shall be filled.' The converse of that beatitude would be: Cursed are they that hunger and thirst after sin; they shall be empty. Your lives are empty because your ultimate appetite is for sin (self-gratification). The more you try to gratify self's appetite; the more self demands. Self's appetite is insatiable. The more sex you get; the more your members demand. You have become slaves to your own lusts. 'You can't get no satisfaction' because there is no satisfaction in sin. You can enjoy the pleasures of sin for a season, but they are fleeting. There will be a day of reckoning; not only in this world but also in the world to come. 'The way of the transgressor is hard.' 'Whatsoever a man sows that will he also reap. For he that soweth to his flesh shall of the flesh reap corruption; but he that soweth to the Spirit shall of the spirit reap life everlasting' " (Galatians 6:8).

Truth has been made obvious to the students. Some become angry because the folly of their selfish lives has been exposed by the swift slash of satire's sword. They are at a point of decision. Either they open their minds and soften their hearts to receive truth, or they will close their minds and harden their hearts. Most will become hardened.

God's Word says: "This is the condemnation, that light (truth) has come into the world, and men love darkness rather than light, because their deeds are evil. For every one that doeth evil hateth the light, neither cometh to the light, lest his deeds should be reproved" (John 3:19, 20).

The mood of the crowd was light hearted when the Mick Jagger imitation was requested but by the end of the illustration the crowd's mood was heavy. Tomorrow students will again ask me to do Mick Jagger. I can not help but wonder if it is not the illustrated truth that they really want to hear.

Our Lord showed that the parable is a priceless instrument for presenting moral lessons. God has given us numerous parables about college life. Like five-year-olds the students beg us to tell the stories over and over. Since the students' lives revolve around sex, booze, drugs and rock 'n roll, I tell many parables that address these sins.

The fraternities are particularly notorious for their licentiousness. I tell the parable of the fraternity boy who boasted of the "good time" he had with a sorority girl. However, when his "good time" resulted in veneral disease and the murder of the offspring of the illicit union, he no longer thought he had such a "good time." The Bible says: "Woe unto them that call evil good, and good evil; they put light for darkness and darkness for light" (Isaiah 5:20).

7

FROM DISCO QUEEN TO GOSPEL PREACHER

"REPENT OF YOUR SINS, YOU WICKED WOMAN," I commanded, pointing at the silly girl who stood in the crowd laughing hysterically as I preached. I never imagined that six years later this girl would become my wife.

Cindy Lasseter was a typical college sophomore when she first heard me preach in December 1977. At the University as a naive freshman and, without any discipline or guidance, she soon fit into the scene of decadence and liberalism. Brother Max and I labeled Cindy the Disco Queen because she was fanatical about dancing and had completed both a twelve-hour and thirty-hour dance-a-thon. She went to the discos at least twice a week.

After I rebuked her, Cindy brought her friends out regularly to listen to Brother Max and me preach the Gospel. They claimed no intention of wanting salvation. To them it was just good entertainment. When I moved on to the next campus, Cindy continued in her sins. As she now reveals, a student did not have to look very far to get involved in sin at the University of

Florida!

Sister Cindy Exposes
The University of Florida

"Beer on tap was sold in at least two places on campus and we could purchase the drinks with our meal tickets. It was unheard of to have a dorm or fraternity party without a keg of beer. Wine and liquor were also commonly used on campus. Students often held what they called 'Bourbon Street Night.' On that evening one hall in the dorm building would become a bar and the residents of each room would serve a different kind of mixed drink. Is it any wonder that both local and national media claim a major problem at UF is alcoholism? The Word says: 'They rise up early in the morning, that they may follow strong drink, and continue until wine inflames them' " (Isaiah 5:11).

"Liquor was not the only tool that UF students used to escape reality. Marijuana, quaaludes, cocaine and other drugs were common. Students often attended class under the influence of these drugs and many were used openly on campus lawns. I even had a friend who grew marijuana in her dorm room.

"Sexual immorality was the norm for most and the number-one sin on campus. The dormitory policies made such practices easy. My building was allowed 24-hour visitation by either sex and all students had the freedom to come and go at any hour. Men and women spent weekends together in the dorm rooms and several times I discovered a resident and her boyfriend taking a shower together in the bathrooms. One prominent woman in Gainesville rightfully labeled the women's dorm, 'Whorehouses.' In God's Word we read: 'Wherefore, God also gave them up to uncleanness through the lusts of their own hearts, to dishonor their own bodies between themselves. For this cause God gave them up unto vile affections; for even the women did exchange the natural use for that which is against nature' (Romans 1:24, 26). My building housed 25 women and six of them were professing lesbians.

"Much of the classroom instruction encouraged this immoral

behavior. The 'Human Sexuality' courses were the first to fill during registration. In this class many hours were spent discussing personal sexual encounters. Other times 'sexologists' lectured on their perverted ideas. They told us that 'premarital sex,' either heterosexual or homosexual, was natural and healthy and that it is perverse and abnormal to resist such desires. The first homework assignment in many of the 'Human Sexuality' classes was to go home, take a mirror and examine our private parts.

"Lust was often the subject in other classes, too. In my speech class a young man chose to talk on streaking. To demonstrate the 'fad' during his speech, three of his fraternity brothers entered the room wearing nothing but tennis shoes. Our female professor laughed the loudest. Also, I had a journalism lab professor who informed the whole class that he was a 'leg man.' He constantly made remarks with sexual connotations to the female students. Another one of my journalism professors admitted to the class that he was 'a dirty old man,' and frequently made lewd remarks in his lectures. A third professor, in the history department, propositioned me in his office one day. I am sure there were some fine upstanding Christian professors at the University of Florida, but in three years I never met one.

"The university infirmary was well-equipped to prepare the students for this lasciviousness. There, all the birth control methods were readily made available. The infirmary also gave pregnancy tests and treated patients with venereal diseases and other such consequences of promiscuity. If a student was found to be with child, she was transferred to an abortion clinic a few blocks off campus. At the clinic, 40-70 unborn babies were murdered each week. Many of the patients were university **students."**

Just a Little Kiss?

Cindy was a junior majoring in journalism and working for the student newspaper when I returned to campus the next year. I quickly noticed her in the crowd but she did not seem to be mocking this time. Later in the week Cindy asked me, "Brother Jed, can I take you out to dinner?"

"No," I answered, "but I will take you. First go home and put on some modest clothes." She was wearing a pair of tight, Sasoon designer jeans.

When Cindy returned wearing a modest skirt, I took her out for a steak dinner. I preached to her the whole time and she seemed open to the things of the Lord. She accompanied me to a revival service that evening but she refused to repent of her sins and commit her life to the Lord Jesus Christ. Convinced that Cindy was ripe for salvation, I invited her to the revival meeting the next night. When I brought her home, we stopped in the parking lot to pray before I walked her to the door.

After our prayer Cindy asked, "Brother Jed, I've heard you say on campus that you haven't kissed a woman in six years. Is that true?"

"Yes, that's correct, Cindy."

"Why, what's wrong with a little kiss?"

"It's not the matter of a little kiss; kisses are important. You don't go around just kissing anyone. The Apostle Paul said, 'It's good for a man not to touch a woman, nevertheless, to avoid fornication let every man have his own wife and let every wife have her own husband'. Cindy, the next woman I kiss will be my bride on my wedding day."

"He's a tough case," Cindy thought to herself as we were both quiet for a minute.

"Why did you ask that, did you want to kiss me?" I inquired.

"Yes."

After Cindy confessed her seductive intentions, I dropped her **at the dorm, IMMEDIATELY. Having hidden the Word of** God in my heart, I was able to resist the temptation. Proverbs 22:14 says, "The mouth of a strange woman is a deep pit."

However, I did take her to church the next day and that afternoon we visited a dear Christian couple, Sid and Ellie Green. They made a good impression on Cindy but she still refused to repent. Even so, the Holy Spirit continued to work on her heart.

Cindy describes what happened when she returned to her dorm room:

"When I got back to my room that afternoon I began to think and cry and to cry and think. I thought about all the divorce in my family and how much sorrow it had brought. Then I recalled the Greens and all the love I had seen in their relationship. Could God have made the difference? Was JESUS the Truth? What is the Truth? The girls in my hall from the Church of Christ said that water baptism was the Truth. The Hare Krishnas and other eastern religionists said that they knew the Truth. Why did I need the Truth, anyway? After all, I was happy. I had found a career that I enjoyed and I had a reasonably secure future. I excelled in dancing. Women in my dorm had told me that they envied my talents. Yes, the devil had fabricated a happiness for me but deep inside I knew that something was missing. Could this JESUS that Jed Smock kept preaching about be the way to happiness? If what he's preaching is the Truth, I thought, I want it. Then I continued to cry."

Conviction and Conversion

That evening I called Cindy and asked her how she was doing.

"Terrible, I've been crying all day and it's your fault."

"It's not my fault, Cindy, it is the Holy Spirit convicting you of your sins. God woke me up early this morning and told me to pray for your conversion because he has a great work for you to do."

"I'm not getting saved," she answered and hung up the phone.

But the next day Cindy was back on campus listening to us preach. Late in the afternoon Brother Max, "Holy Hubert" Lindsey and I were going over to the Krystal Hamburger Restaurant and I invited Cindy to go along. While we were eating, Brother Max asked her why she was not a Christian.

"I just don't have any faith," she replied.

The fact is her mind had been blinded to the truth by the lies of the evolutionists, socialists, humanists and perverts of the university system.

Brother Max suggested that Cindy pray for faith and she agreed. The four of us went outside, held hands and began to pray. I led Cindy in a sinner's prayer of repentance toward God and faith in Jesus Christ.

On New Year's Day I baptized her in the Gulf of Mexico. Soon afterwards the words "GO YE AND PREACH" came to Cindy in a vision. But she returned to school, continued her job with the newspaper and almost forgot the incident. At school Cindy continued to seek God with her whole heart. She describes in her own words how God made her call to preach clear:

Called to Preach

"I desired to know God better every day. One night as I read the Gospel of Luke, I asked JESUS if there was anything else He would have me read. Instantly, he said, 'II Timothy 4:2.' Unfamiliar with the scripture, I turned the pages of my Bible once and it fell open to that passage. 'Preach the word . . .' Afraid to read further, I snapped my Bible shut. A rush of power shot through my heart and I almost fainted. A few minutes later I read the rest of the scripture, 'Preach the word; be diligent in season, out of season: reprove, rebuke, exhort with all long-suffering and doctrine.' I knew God had called me to preach."

At the time, Cindy was top reporter for the student newspaper. She had been interviewed by the state's leading newspapers and seemed to have a promising career in journalism — but God had other plans for her. He soon led her to quit working for the newspaper and put her in The Campus Ministry.

She recalls:

"The second week in February I was fasting and received my first sermon from Isaiah 55. God told me to go out on the 'Plaza of the Americas' at the University of Florida and deliver the message to the students. So two and one-half months after Jesus saved me, I entered the battlefield with these words, 'Ho, everyone that thirsteth, come to the waters, and he that hath no money; come, buy and eat; yea, come buy wine and milk without money and without price . . .' My preaching was quite a shock and a wonderful testimony to the student body, especially Brother Jed's regular mockers who knew me as a fellow heckler. At that very spot a few months earlier I had mocked God's Word. But now I was a new creature. Old things had passed away. Behold, all things had become new.

"I began going out regularly witnessing and preaching to the students. Day after day the Holy Spirit would remind me of John 4:35, 'Say not ye, There are yet four months and then cometh the Harvest? Behold I say unto you, Lift up your eyes and look on the fields; for they are white already to harvest."

"In May, God called me to quit school and begin harvesting the college and university campuses."

Cindy Joins the Destroyers

That month Cindy joined Brother Max and me in Ohio. She got initiated into the Campus Ministry at Bowling Green State University. The three of us had been preaching on campus all week and had been holding nightly meetings in a local church. Sunday was our last day in the city and we rarely went on campus on Sundays. But as we were coming back from lunch after church, Cindy looked at the campus and saw a crowd of students lying in the sun near a pond. The girls were lying out in their bikini bathing suits and the boys were next to them in cut-offs. The Lord spoke to her heart telling her to preach to those students. She put on her hat, grabbed her Bible and marched over to the pond.

The Lord told Cindy what to say to get their attention: "Hearken unto the word of God. I've got a message for you people from God: GET YOUR CLOTHES ON! Not only are you physically naked but more important your hearts are naked. God can see right into your evil hearts and they are an abomination in his sight. Unless you repent of your sins and believe in

Jesus, you're never going to be happy in this life or the life after."

That got their attention. They jumped up from their towels and blankets and others came out of their dorm rooms and gathered around. Before long Cindy was preaching to a crowd of 150. After about 15 minutes the police came up and suggested Cindy leave.

"Why? Don't I have freedom of speech?" she asked.

"Yes, but we have gotten about six phone calls that they're going to throw you in that pond if you don't stop preaching. We just want you to know that we won't give you any protection," a policeman answered.

Despite the threat, Cindy continued speaking. Suddenly, four boys grabbed her, swung her three times and threw her into the pond. That little bit of water could not put out the Holy Spirit Fire! Cindy leaped from that pond covered in mud and soaked in water and continued to preach the Gospel of Jesus Christ.

Later, one student said, "That sure was powerful — you coming out of that pond like that."

"Well, I serve a powerful God!" Cindy exclaimed.

When she returned and told me the whole story, I decided to go preach to that gang of rebels. By now they were back in their dorms. I shouted up to their windows, "You sissies and pansies who threw an innocent woman into the pond, come out here and listen to the Word of God."

They flooded out of their rooms and surrounded me. After a few minutes of preaching they tried to throw me into the pond but a girl came up and insisted they stop.

Meanwhile, Cindy was witnessing to one who had been a constant heckler that week. He accepted her invitation to church and at the end of the service he went to the altar confessing his sins and calling upon the name of the Lord. The pastor remarked that he was going to take Cindy and throw her in that pond several times a day to bring in some more lost souls!

This was the beginning of the great plans that God had for Cindy — a ministry that would shake the university campuses of America. That fall she started preaching on campuses in the

Midwest and in the winter she preached across the southern states from Florida to California. I rejoiced at the way this 20-year-old girl fearlessly entered strange cities and single-handedly invaded campus after campus. Cindy was faithful about preaching at least four days a week, several hours a day. In four years she ministered on 85 universities in 25 states.

Some of the impact of Cindy's ministry is revealed in a Humboldt State University student's account of her visit to his California campus. The following paper is just one of many that has been written and submitted to professors about our ministry:

The Miraculous Sister Cindy

"What an absolutely incredible, righteously, wonderful thing to do — to stand up and hit'em with both barrels, to boldly and forthrightly deliver the Gospel message to a sick and ailing bunch of losers. With no punches pulled, not the watered-down Christian type of sermonizing we've all heard before; yes, 'hell-fire and damnation,' but with the archer's arrow striking home. Sister Cindy preached salvation for four-and-a-half hours straight in the most truthful and moving way I have ever heard. Such truth coming from the mouth of a moral and virtuous woman was a delight to my ears. She is a gift from God, truly a jewel amongst the broken fragments of humanity. I could scarcely believe my eyes and ears as I walked up to the jeering and laughing crowd at the Art Center square Thursday, May 19, 1983. She came unto the so-called educated and they knew her not.

"I was walking up to Founders Hall when I heard the commotion coming from the Art Center. To my surprise a young lady dressed in a brown skirt, white blouse and a light brown hat was preaching repentance and salvation to a crowd of unbelievers. A majority of them were making fun of her and a few individuals were vehemently trying to dispute her and upset her but all attempts were to no avail. Cindy's delivery was so sure and true that all her tormentors appeared to be nothing but a pack of fools. Fools is only a beginning description of the crowd.

When Cindy Lasseter hit those students with the truth and told them exactly what they are they proved it beyond a shadow of doubt by their reactions. They behaved like animals. I guess you can't expect much more from people when you consider that college teaches them 'we are animals.'

"Miss Lasseter's flare for speaking, her animated and humorous personality and her innocent childlike demeanor came through to reach everyone present that day, sinners and saved alike. To me, she reached the very core of my soul, and made my spirit sing; to others she inflamed their hatred, resentment or rebellion. The crowd was having their fun through mimicry — more and more as the day wore on; but her courage will always be impressed upon my memory.

"Webster's New World Dictionary (Second College Edition 1970) defines the word 'fornication' as: 'voluntary sexual intercourse, generally forbidden by law, between an unmarried man and woman;' and the word 'whore': 'any woman who engages in promiscuous sexual intercourse,' and the word 'whoremonger': 'a man who fornicates or associates with whores.' Today in our society there are no laws governing morality; anything goes; but God's laws coincide with Webster's Dictionary.

"Well, there you have it. So all 'hell' broke loose when Sister Cindy pointed her finger and accused those who engaged in casual sexual intercourse, and those who are living together unmarried of whoring and whoremongering. 'You whores and whoremongers, unless you repent and turn from your ways, you are headed for hell. The reason you don't repent is because you love your wicked ways,' she said hitting the students right where they live.

"Cindy Lasseter was giving those lost individuals a chance to look at themselves; but they scorned her, streaked naked in front of her, tried to out-shout her, tried to woo her into accepting a rose in the name of peace and love (phony), and even tried to physically pull her down off the little cement water fountain structure that she was speaking from. But Sister Cindy's spirit was indomitable. All the charades of silly people masquerading in reaction to the Word of God could not shake the Holy Spirit or that dear Saint, Cindy Lasseter. All those clowns of Satan trying to steal the show failed miserably; they fell away to the left, they fell away to the right, and those trying to upstage her in front faded in her brightness; for you see, the one in the center spotlight, Cindy, was the greatest of all; none of her competitors could hold a candle to her: Cindy's brightness out-shown them all.

"She came with love and concern but none the less with sword for the lost sinners that day. Oh, she wielded that sword majestically, not once faltering or missing a cue all afternoon. Did they receive her? Some believed that she was a theater arts major giving a performance. They didn't know what she was saying, or realize that the message behind Cindy's theatrics was deadly serious. They didn't know what they were doing; they came to destroy, and to cut her down, but I think she secretly won the hearts of many. I seriously doubt that there ever has been a person at Humboldt State University who has moved an audience to the depth of their emotions. Quite an attraction, Cindy was. Rolls of film were shot; there was non-stop video tape coverage, and even the local TV station captured this little miracle worker in action.

"The negative reaction to Cindy has pained my heart, but now I see the miracle that she has already performed. No one can deny the truth that she spoke; they may choose to admit or ignore it. However, Cindy's message is lodged somewhere in their hearts and minds. Who knows what will happen the next time she shows up on campus?"

By Sam Trumbull

What is wrong with Brother Jed,
doesn't he like me anymore? He
hasn't rebuked me once this year.
— Coed at the University of Florida

8

OPEN REBUKE
IS BETTER...

When I was speaking at the University of Wisconsin at LaCrosse, I invited a local associate pastor and youth leader to campus. Initially, he was very enthusiastic about my ministry. However, as the crowd (including many professing Christians) vehemently turned against me, he sided with them. He led the throng in denouncing me and he jumped up on my makeshift platform and renounced me as a false prophet. Since he had gained the crowd's attention, the expedient thing was for me to step down and let him have his say. He summed up his brief message on "love" with an invitation: "You come to First Church Sunday morning. We won't PREACH to you!"

I was infuriated when this so-called full gospel pastor told them they would not hear PREACHING at his church. I leaped on a bench, rebuked the pastor and began to PREACH harder than ever. Eventually I regained the crowd's attention but the pastor continued fighting against the work of God through the next day.

Like most ministers, this man allowed the world to determine his approach to evangelism. At first he had thought my preaching was great but when he saw the students respond with mockery and ridicule he became discouraged and decided "there must be a better way."

The church has heard the world say, "This preaching turns us off, don't preach to us!" So Christians on campus try "rap" sessions, debates on evolution versus creation, book tables, distribution of tracts, Christian movies, contemporary Christian singing groups or picnics — anything but preaching. Can you imagine the apostles going to Corinth or Athens and setting up a book table?

The Bible says, "It pleased God by the foolishness of PREACHING to save them that believe" (I Corinthians 1:21).

Jesus said, "Go into all the world and PREACH the gospel to every creature. He that believeth and is baptized shall be saved, but he that believeth not shall be damned" (Mark 16:15, 16).

"What ye hear in the ear, PREACH ye upon the housetop" (Mark 10:27).

"God manifested his word through PREACHING" (Titus 1:3).

"How shall they hear without a PREACHER?" (Romans 10:14).

Yet many who name the name of Christ are not only ashamed of preaching but fiercely oppose public proclamation of the message of repentance "toward God and faith toward our Lord Jesus."

"For the PREACHING of the cross is to them that perish, foolishness; but unto us that are saved it is the power of God" (I Corinthians 1:18).

True Christians should not be discouraged when they see the world regard preaching as foolishness. This is precisely the response the Holy Spirit warned that we would receive. The apostles were regularly mocked, ridiculed, spat upon, mobbed, beaten, imprisoned, stoned and martyred. To a degree all of these things have happened to us on campus. Jesus said to his unbelieving kindred, "The world cannot hate you; but me it hateth, because I testify of it, that the works thereof are evil" (John 7:7).

Paul said, "Have no fellowship with the unfruitful works of darkness, but rather reprove them" (Ephesians 5:11). Only when Christians begin to cry out against everything that is wicked and evil in this generation will there be revival. The church wants to be loved and accepted by the world.

Jesus said: "If you were of the world, the world would love his own: but because you are not of the world, but I have chosen you out of the world, therefore the world hateth you. Remember the word that I said unto you, The servant is not greater than his Lord. If they have persecuted me, they will also persecute you" (John 15:18, 19).

Away with this friendship approach to evangelism! Let us love people enough to warn, reprove and rebuke them for their sins, risking their rejection.

But some argue, "You will turn them off." I say, they are already off. Indeed, we do drive most of them even further away. But so did Jesus, who remarked, "If I had not come and spoken unto them, they had not had sin: But now they have no cloak for their sin."

Charles G. Finney, one of America's greatest evangelists, taught that preachers were to expose all the sinner's hiding places and take sides with God against sin. Many "Christians," like the pastor I met in LaCrosse, side with the sinner against God. These hyprocrites are hiding their own sins with a cloak of sympathy. My purpose is to rip off every transgressor's cloak and bare them stark naked before God and man. When they discover their nakedness, most, like Adam, will vainly attempt to hide from God. But a few, like the woman at the well, will seek for the garments of salvation and the robes of righteousness.

Most people were worse off after hearing Jesus because they rejected what he had to say. Those who hear the Word will either open their hearts to it or harden their hearts. The Bible makes clear that most will harden their hearts: "For wide is the gate, and broad is the way, that leadeth to destruction, and many there be which go in thereat. Because strait is the gate, and narrow is the way, which leadeth unto life, and few there be that find it" (Matthew 7:13, 14).

Regardless of how much evidence men are confronted with most will refuse to believe the claims of Christianity because believing requires men to forsake their sins. Jesus said: "And this is the condemnation, that light is come into the world, and men loved darkness rather than light, because their deeds were evil. For everyone that doeth evil hateth the light, neither cometh to the light, lest his deeds should be reproved" (John 3:19, 20).

The last thing the sinner wants to do is give up his sins for he loves sin and hates righteousness. If we are going to be successful in bringing a revival to America, we must do just the opposite. We must love righteousness and hate sin.

The Key to Jesus' Success

According to the Father, the key to Jesus' powerful anointing was that he "loved righteousness, and hated iniquity" (Hebrews 1:9). But, alas, men who profess to follow Christ have come to tolerate and excuse sin in their own lives, in the church and in the world and only do mouth service to righteousness. Paul wrote: "Awake unto righteousness and sin not; for some have not the knowledge of God: I speak this to your shame" (I Corinthians 15:34). If we are going to have the Lord's anointing it will take much more than the laying on of hands. We must meet the condition of loving righteousness and hating iniquity.

The Key to Paul's Success

Paul said, "Knowing therefore the terror of the Lord, we persuade men" (II Corinthians 5:11). If we are going to successfully bring men to repentance and faith we must know the terror, the fear, the wrath of an angry God against this rebellious generation.

Paul saw multitudes and multitudes in the valley of decision about to fall into the pit of hell. He knew the terror of the Lord! There needs to be a revival of the knowledge of the "wrath of God which is revealed from heaven against all ungodliness and unrighteousness of men, who hold the truth in unrighteousness (Romans 1:18).

Jesus forewarned us, "Fear him, which after he hath killed, hath power to cast unto hell; yea, I say unto you, Fear God!" (Luke 12:5). Even Jesus feared his Father (Hebrews 5:7). If the only begotten Son feared God, how much more should we, his adopted sons, fear him? Remember that: "By faith, Noah, being warned of God of things not seen as yet, moved with fear, prepared an ark to the saving of his house; by which he condemned the world, and became heir of the righteousness which is by faith" (Hebrews 11:7).

Jesus, Paul and Noah were not only motivated by love more than anyone, but the fear of God also propelled them. This generation knows not the fear of the Lord.

Just what is the fear of God?

W.E. Vine's dictionary defines it as more than a "fear of his power and righteous retribution, but a wholesome dread of displeasing him."

"The fear of the Lord is to hate evil" (Proverbs 8:13). Those that fear God "love righteousness and hate iniquity."

Since the church is so ignorant of the fear of God, it lacks wisdom and understanding. It lacks the burning zeal that motivated Jesus, the apostles and the prophets of old.

The leading minister in the Colonial Awakening was Jonathan Edwards. Large numbers of New Englanders were enormously stirred by his best known sermon "Sinners in the Hands of an Angry God" — a sermon on the painfully suggestive text "Their foot shall slide in due time." The message usually resulted in great distress and weeping as sinners were deeply impressed and bowed down with an awful conviction of sin and its dangers.

When Felix listened to Paul concerning faith in Christ, he trembled as Paul reasoned of "righteousness, temperance, and judgment to come." Oh, that men would once again tremble upon hearing the WORD. They will when the truth is proclaimed. The Word says "Preach the word; be instant in season, out of season; reprove, rebuke, exort with all long suffering and doctrine" (II Timothy 4:12).

Exorcism

Evangelicals emphazise Mark's account of the Great Commission of Jesus Christ to his disciples to "Go into all the world and preach the gospel." But most of them stop at preaching. They exclude Jesus' final promise, included in Mark's account, that certain signs would follow believers:

As we travel the campuses we pray for God to confirm his Word with signs. One day while I was preaching at Princeton University a women's "libber" who had been contending with me all afternoon was suddenly grabbed by a wild-eyed male student who began cursing her and shouting "Get thee to hell! Get thee to hell!"

The following day the student newspaper gave a vivid account of what happened next:

> Several onlookers attempted to restrain the attacker while Smock began to speak in Latin. The assailant continued to struggle and shout until Smock commanded him to stop "in the name of Jesus Christ." On hearing that, the assaulter dropped his hands to his sides and said, "Okay."

My command gave the whole campus tangible evidence to the authority of the name of Jesus over devils.

The assailant quickly left the scene and the distraught female was comforted by her friends. Several minutes later security officers arrived, concluded that I was the source of the problem and ordered me to leave campus. Since it was late in the day, I did not question their authority.

The next day I met with the dean of students to get permission to return to campus. He had a letter prepared for me stating that I was "persona non grata" at Princeton University and threatened me with arrest should I return. When I attempted to reason with the dean, I discovered that he had no fear of God and was ignorant of spiritual things. He informed me that the attacker did not remember a thing about the incident. The dean thought that I had power over the demons rather than the student. The assailant recalled nothing that happened because evil spirits had taken control of his mind until I cast them out in Jesus' name.

I left the campus to preach at Rutgers University that afternoon. For days after I pondered what Jonathan Edwards, who was one of Princeton's early presidents, would have thought if he were aware of the spiritual darkness that exists at the university today.

The Law of Love

Like Jonathan Edwards I am known as a hell fire and brimstone preacher. Many professing Christians object that I am preaching too much on God's wrath and judgment.

One day a girl said to me, "You need to tell those students how much God loves them — that is what they need to hear."

I addressed the crowd of about 200 and asked, "How many agree with her?" Almost everyone raised their hands. Whereupon I responded, "If you are convinced God loves you, how come you are not serving him?"

The crowd quieted down. Another question, "How many believe anyone who is not a Christian is going to hell?" Very few hands went up. One more question, "How many believe that Jesus hates sin?" Even fewer hands went up. I turned to the girl and said, "This is what they need to hear. They have heard your message of love and refused it so I must warn them that they are going to get God's wrath and judgment."

Certainly, the Bible teaches that "God is love" but the scriptures also describe our God as a "consuming fire." Few people realize that the wrath and judgment of God against sin is a manifestation of his love. It is more important to be motivated by LOVE than to preach about LOVE. God's Word says: "My little children let us not love in word, neither in tongue, but in deed and in truth" (I John 3:18).

Jesus was motivated by love but he only speaks of God's love for humanity in six verses of the four Gospels. In 163 verses he speaks of wrath, hell, condemnation and judgment. Nowhere in the Book of Acts is the love of God even mentioned but the fear of God is referred to six times.

The real issue facing the world and the church is not the fact that God loves humanity. Very few people deny this. The real question is does humanity love God? A popular poster in hippie pads of the 60s proclaimed, "God is love." The love of God generally proclaimed to this generation is not the love of God at all but a humanistic love presented in the name of God.

The test of real love is given by our Lord Jesus Christ "If ye love me, keep my commandments" (John 14:15). "This is the love of God that we keep his commandments" (I John 5:3).

Those who love God will obey God. Those who obey him not, love him not. They may have emotional feelings for God but if their love does not produce obedience then they are lost in their trespasses and sins and headed for HELL.

A popular tract used on campus is called "The Four Spiritual Laws." It cannot be denied that this tract has been used to win souls, however it has serious weaknesses that have produced counterfeit conversions. A study of Jesus' methods of evangelism shows the fallacies of this witnessing tool. The chief problem with the tract is that it professes to be presenting laws to bring people to the Lord but it ignores the moral law of God which the Bible says "is our schoolmaster to lead us to Christ" (Galatians 3:24).

Considering the first "law" the tract shares will illustrate my point. It says, "God loves you and offers a wonderful plan for your life." The statement God loves you is a spiritual truth but it is not the moral law of God which the scriptures say shows a man his need for the Savior.

Jesus summed up the moral law by preaching what could be called the two spiritual laws.

One day a lawyer asked Jesus, "Master, which is the great commandment in the law?"

Jesus said unto him, "Thou shalt love the Lord thy God with all thy heart, and with all thy soul, and with all thy mind. This is the first and great commandment, and the second is like unto it, Thou shalt love thy neighbor as thyself. On these two commandments hang all the law and the prophets" (Matthew 22:37-40).

Love God supremely and your neighbor equally. This is what the Bible is all about and it was the emphasis in Jesus' teaching. Contemporary evangelism has separated God's love from his law. This is one of the oldest heresies in Christendom: antinomianism. The result has been humanism in the name of Christ. This has intensified the lawlessness and rebellion of this generation and comforted the sinner in his sins.

Like Jesus, modern evangelists should emphasize man's duty to God and his neighbor. It is the moral (spiritual) law of God that must be taught the sinner.

Martin Luther in his Preface to Romans writes, "The first duty of the Gospel preacher is to declare God's law and show the nature of sin." He was convinced that a man would never see his Savior until he saw his sin!

But some disagree and say: "You don't have to tell unbelievers they are sinners; they already know that."

I say, if they know, then they have not learned much at school because the humanistic philosophy has brainwashed students, teaching that men are naturally good. The Bible instructs that men are basically evil because they are in rebellion against God. Sin is not in the vocabulary of this perverse generation. Even students who will acknowledge wrongdoing still believe that they are basically moral people whose good deeds outweigh their bad deeds. The evangelist must impress on them that they are wicked to the core. There is not anything good about them. All their righteousness is as filthy rigs in the sight of a holy GOD.

The law brings the sinner to a knowledge of sin. Paul said: "Now we know that what things soever the law saith, it saith to them who are under the law: that every mouth may be stopped and all the world may become guilty before God . . . for by the law is the knowledge of sin" (Romans 3:19, 20).

Paul described the work of the law in his own pre-conversion experience, "But sin, seizing the opportunity afforded by the commandment, produced in me every kind of covetous desire . . ." (Romans 7:8). He added "I had not known lust, except the law had said, Thou shalt not covet" (Romans 7:7).

As I preach God's commandments on campus it brings out the worst in my audience because the law reaches deep into the sinner's heart and pulls out his true motives.

God's Garbage Man

Three graduate students, puzzled by the antagonism of the students, invited me out to dinner when I was speaking at the University of Southern Illinois.

One of them said to me, "Brother Jed, we have been listening to you preach since we were freshmen. We have always wanted to ask you why the students behave as they do when you preach to them. Normally, they aren't that bad. We recognize that they are sinners but usually they aren't as gross, lewd and disrespectful as they are when you preach. We can't figure out their behavior. We room with them, eat and study with them. Usually they aren't like that. Could you explain their behavior?"

"Yes, I can. Your sinner is like a garbage can," I replied. "Basically, there are two types of sinners. One represented by a garbage can which is painted nicely, without a dent, which always has its lid on. This is your sinner who has actually come to college to get an education and does not spend his substance in reveling and riotous living. The second sinner is represented by a can in which the paint is chipped with dents on the side with a lid that is often ajar. This represents most students who have come to college because it's a good place to party while someone else foots the bill. He spends his time in drunkenness and debauchery. Both sinners try to keep the lids on their cans because they want to leave the impression that they are basically good people. They try to cover their sins. The first sinner is much more conscientious about covering his sins than the second. But both cans are filled with garbage. Their sin is always present with them.

I continued, "You might call me God's garbage man. I come in the power of the Holy Spirit and with the law of God pull the lids off their cans. All the stench and stink of sin comes fuming out. As God's garbage man I make a lot of noise and commotion. I turn the cans upside down and shake out the refuse. Finally, I take the water of the Gospel and hose them out. Gentlemen, you are seeing the students for what they truly are but most of the time they cover up their rottenness."

Admittedly, my ministry brings out the worst in people. But some, at the end of the day, will return to the privacy of their rooms and reflect on their behavior with shame. For the first time they will see themselves for what they actually are — decadent, depraved and degenerate.

The sinner to be saved must admit to more than wrongdoing. He must see how utterly malignant, cunning, repulsive, deadly and damnable his sin is. Until he realizes the exceeding sinfulness of sin, he will never see the great love of his Saviour. The sinner must be convinced that he has stood against God. Realizing this, some may try to reform but eventually they will recognize their failure to be righteous.

My duty is to thrust in the sword until the sinner cries "O wretched man that I am! What must I do to be saved? How shall I escape from the bondage of sin?"

Only at this point can the sinner appreciate the precious atonement of our Lord Jesus Christ. Desperate for deliverance he will throw himself upon Christ for salvation from the slavery of sin.

Then my purpose is accomplished: these cans of garbage are transformed into "vessels unto honor, sanctified, and meet for the Master's use, and prepared unto every good work" (II

Timothy 2:12).

Name Calling

Sister Cindy has often reflected, "The kindest thing anyone ever said to me was when Jed Smock said, 'Repent of your sins, you wicked woman.' This was the first time anyone ever told me the truth about myself."

There is an old adage, "The truth hurts." But actually it is the lie that hurts, destroys and kills. The truth heals, the truth sets free, the truth brings life. Granted, the truth has sting to it.

A common criticism of our ministry is our name calling. Labeling individuals as whores, whoremongers, perverts, queers, drunkards, dope fiends, wimps, etc. We have been accused of saying that all students fall into one or more of these categories or that all fraternity boys are drunkards and all sorority girls are whores.

"You are generalizing," our critics cry.

"Sure we are generalizing," I repy, "but a generalization by definition implies exceptions." Of course there are morally upright college students but the fact is that most are engaging in gross sin.

The last taboo is for an individual to tell people what they are doing is wicked and sinful and condemns. them. Regretably, most Christians have come to honor this taboo. They will sometimes say, "I can show you a better way of living," but rarely would they say to the crowd, "You are wicked, sinful and condemned." They know not the Proverb, "Faithful are the wounds of a friend, but the kisses of an enemy are deceitful" (Proverbs 27:6).

Jesus called individuals names and condemned people. He called the King a fox. He called two of his disciples devils. He referred to a gentile woman as a dog. He exposed the unbelieving Jews as children of the devil. He called the religious leaders "vipers, hypocrites, blind guides, fools, and whitewashed tombs." Not only does Jesus rebuke and condemn individuals and groups but he declares his generation to be "faithless and perverse and adulterous." He curses whole cities "Woe unto you Chorazin, Bethsaida, Capernaum" (Matthew 11:21-24). Finally, he curses the world: "Woe unto the world because of offenses" (Matthew 18:7).

At the University of Florida there was an exceptionally attractive coed named Judy who was also very lewd and vulgar. As a rule we do not point out individuals unless they first challenge what we are saying and publicly confess to their sin without shame. Judy was a gross sinner and wanted everyone to know it. Therefore, each year I would rebuke her personally and use her as an example of what a woman should not be. Her junior year, however, I ignored her. One day, desperate for attention, dressed in her typical attire of short, short-shorts, she added a T-shirt with an obscene word on the front. Again I ignored her. At the end of the day she asked Cindy, "What is wrong with Brother Jed, doesn't he like me anymore? He hasn't rebuked me once this year."

Proverbs 27:5 says, "Open rebuke is better than secret love."

Jesus had enough love for the rich young ruler that he put his finger on his sin of covetousness. When are Christians going to show enough love for the lost to follow Christ's example of ministry?

Judging

When shown the scriptures our critics will admit that Jesus called names, then they argue, "But you're not Jesus."

"The Bible shows you utterly ignorant," I reply. "He that sayeth he abideth in Christ ought himself also to walk, even as He walked!" (I John 2:6).

"Now you're judging us," they puff.

"Judge not, judge not," they scream. "The Bible says not to judge."

"Quote on, sinners! You know part of one whole Bible verse; now quote the following verses and put it in its context."

Usually, Matthew 7:1 is quoted to me several times a day. I have never met a sinner who cannot quote at least part of it. Nor have I ever met a sinner who is able to accept my challenge to put the verse in its context.

Let us examine the entire passage:

"Judge not that ye be not judged. For with what judgment ye judge, ye shall be judged; and with what measure ye mete, it shall be measured to you again. And why beholdst thou the mote that is in thy brother's eye, but considereth not the beam that is in thine own eye? Or how will thou say to thy brother, Let me pull out the mote out of thine eye; and behold, a beam is in thine own eye? Thou hypocrite, first cast out the beam out of thine own eye and then thou shalt clearly to cast out the mote out of thy brother's eye" (Matthew 7:1-5).

Notice that "judge not" is NOT a universal admonition; it is directed to the hypocrite — one who condemns others for what he himself does (Romans 2:3). The Lord is rebuking hypocrites for their unfair judgments. The beam symbolizes sin. The believer by faith in Christ has cast the beam out of his eye or the sin out of the lives of others because his judgment is no longer blurred by his own sin. In the same chapter Jesus warns us, "Beware of false prophets" (verse 15). How can we recognize a false messenger if we do not judge?

Many who piously quote, "Judge not," do not see their own inconsistency in condemning those who judge righteously.

The Lord Jesus commanded, "Judge righteous judgment" (John 7:24). He told a man, "Thou hast rightly judged" (Luke 7:43). To others our Lord asked, "Why even of yourselves judge ye not what is right?" (Luke 12:57).

The Apostle Paul wrote, "He that is spiritual judgeth all things" (I Corinthians 2:15). Paul reminded us, "Do ye not know that the saints (Christians) shall judge the world? Know ye not we shall judge angels? How much more things that pertain to this life" (I Corinthians 6:23).

In fact, it is our duty and responsibility to judge according to the truth of God's Word. We must "Abhor that which is evil; cleave to that which is good" (Romans 12:9).

Indeed, God has given us the Bible so that we might judge right from wrong, good from evil and truth from error.

But students cry the more, "You are condemning us, you are condemning us, Jesus did not condemn the woman caught in adultery."

In John 8 we have one of the best known and most misunderstood stories in the Bible. In this narrative our basic message is simply illustrated. "Make Jesus your Lord, and stop sinning."

Admittedly Jesus did not condemn this woman but throughout the gospels we do find him condemning the scribes and Pharisees. He warned them, "Ye serpents, ye generation of vipers, how can ye escape the damnation of hell?" (Matthew 23:33). Why did Jesus not condemn the woman but so often condemn the scribes and Pharisees? Did he love them less? No. The Pharisees refused to repent and believe in the Lord, whereas the woman repented.

When Jesus asked her, "Hath no man condemned thee?" She said, "No man, Lord."

This repentance — calling on the Lord Jesus out of a sincere heart. Paul wrote: "If you shalt confess with thy mouth the Lord Jesus, and shalt believe in thine heart that God hath raised him from the dead, thou shalt be saved. For with the heart man believeth unto righteousness; and with the mouth confession is made unto salvation. For whosoever shall call on the name of the Lord shall be saved" (Romans 10:9, 10, 13).

This woman did not try to defend or excuse her sinful behavior as so many students do when we confront them. She knew she had done wrong and was willing to change or Jesus would never have forgiven her. Jesus did not condemn her because, through her faith in the Lord, she believed with her heart unto righteousness.

The scribes and Pharisees, in contrast, walked away, each convicted by their own consciences which told them that they were wrong; but still they refused to repent and believe. They refused to follow Jesus. So it is with most students. The Word of God convicts their consciences, showing them their sins. But instead of repenting most, sooner or later, walk away. Some stay around and ask questions to test us. Others will mock or heckle.

They will do anything but repent.

When some see that mocking and heckling does not discourage us they resort to violence, like Cain who slew his brother. The Bible says "And wherefore he slew him? Because his own works were evil and his brother's were righteous" (I John 3:12).

*It is a fine sight to see a
minister of the Gospel marched off
by the servant of the law.
— Charles Spurgeon*

9

MOCKED, MOBBED, BEATEN, STONED AND IMPRISONED

"Brother Jed, since you have been on this campus you have been mocked, ridiculed, spat upon, shoved and even had a pie thrown in your face. I understand on other campuses you have been punched and arrested. Do you ever get fearful for you life?" asked a reporter who interviewed me at Ohio University.

"Young man," I answered, "In the days of the Wild West in Dodge City, Kansas, there was a cemetary called Boot Hill. It was called Boot Hill because they used to bury (with their boots on) the gunslingers who shot one another in the streets. This is how I want to go. With my guns a-blazen and my boots on!"

At another university a dear Christian sister tearfully said, "Brother Jed, I feel so badly for you when I consider the way you have been treated on this campus."

"Oh sister!" I replied, "You should not feel that way. The Apostle Peter explained, 'If ye be reproached for the name of Christ, happy are ye; for the spirit of glory and of God resteth upon you: on their part He is evil spoken of, but on your part He is glorified' (I Peter 4:14). The more the students insult me, the more of his glory God bestows upon me. They are speaking evil of God but all the more God is being glorified through me."

Jesus encouraged us when he said, "Blessed are ye, when men shall hate you, and when they shall separate you from their company, and shall reproach you, and cast out your name as evil, for the son of man's sake. Rejoice ye in that day, and leap for joy: for behold, your reward is great in heaven: for in like manner did their fathers unto the prophets" (Luke 6:22, 23).

Her tears turned into laughter as I began to joyfully leap and jump.

If the prophets were persecuted for their faith, why should we expect different treatment in the 20th century? Paul exhorted young Timothy, "Stir up the gift of God, which is in thee by the putting on of my hands." We need to rekindle the inner power of the Holy Spirit that is within us and not be afraid or ashamed to testify about our Lord. We are admonished: "Be thou a partaker of the afflictions of the gospel," Paul exhorted (II Timothy 1:6, 8). In this generation we have majored in the blessing of the good news; it is time we at least minor in the sufferings of the Gospel.

The Word teaches us: "By faith, Moses, when he was come to years, refused to be called the son of Pharaoh's daughter" (Hebrews 11:24). He disdained to be considered a "King's Kid." It is high time baby Christians grow up like Moses who chose "to suffer affliction with the people of God" (verse 25). Instead, so-called Christians are choosing the comforts of this world seeking respectability and rejecting the crucified life. Moses esteemed "the reproach of Christ greater riches than all the treasures in Egypt" (verse 26). Today's "believers" exercise their faith to appropriate the wealth of Egypt (the things of this world — new cars, a bigger salary, a new house) and scorn the stigma of the Gospel.

I heard a Lutheran clergyman say, "In America we don't suffer persecution because we live in a country that has religious freedom." He was right about the fact but wrong about the reason. Indeed, there are few who are suffering persecution for their faith because most who profess the name of Christ are not taking the kind of stand that they ought. The Bible says: "Yea, and all that will live godly in Christ Jesus shall suffer persecution" (II Timothy 3:12). Instead of persecution they seek the soft flesh life-style.

When believers live holy and separated lives, persecution will surely come their way. For example, parents and preachers, who have exercised their inalienable right to separate their children from a God-rejecting state school system, have been jailed in America. Churches have been padlocked because pastors refused to bow their knees to Caesar. Christians have been arrested for demonstrating against baby murdering factories called abortion clinics. While many college professors openly mock God and deride Christians in the classroom, my associate Max Lynch was fired by Indiana State University for reading the Bible to his students. Alas, the Lutheran minister was essentially correct — examples of persecution are exceptional. Most who profess to be Christians are not bothered by the world because they do not bother the world.

Jailed in Indianapolis

Although the main thrust of my ministry has been the university campus, I have preached in front of high schools, on main streets, public beaches, at county fairs and at rock concerts. Generally one may preach in public places without hinderance from the authorities. Although the Constitution guarantees free speech in public places, sometimes local police fail to recognize this right. As a result I have been arrested on so many occassions over the years that I lost count a long time ago.

One day I was preaching on Monument Circle in downtown Indianapolis, Indiana. A policeman interrupted me and said that a permit was required to preach on the city streets. It is important to cooperate with the authorities, if possible. Therefore, I went to the city controller and he informed me that a permit was not needed to preach on the public street, because this was a constitutional right. Quickly I returned to Monument Circle but a jazz rock group with loud amplifiers was playing on the steps of the Episcopalian Church. The demonic chords resounded around the circle. I was angry that God's building was being dishonored by Satan's minstrels. About a hundred people had gathered to listen. When they played their last song I walked on to the church yard, pointed my finger at the musicians and church and pronounced judgment crying, "Ichabod — the glory is departed from this church!"

I stepped back to the public sidewalk and continued preaching to the crowd. The priest, flowing in his gown, came out to investigate and I sharply rebuked him for permitting the building to be used by the devil. He ran back into the church and evidently called the police because in a few minutes two squad cars came screeching to the curb. The police again insisted that I needed a permit to preach. I replied that the city controller had said that a permit was not necessary. The police then commanded me to stop speaking.

But I responded as Peter and John did when they were ordered to stop preaching in Jerusalem: "Whether it be right in the sight of God to hearken unto you more than unto God, judge ye. For I cannot but speak the things which I have seen and heard' " (Acts 4:19, 20).

The police then threatened me with arrest. Again, I answered as the apostles, "I ought to obey God rather than men" (Acts 5:29). However, they thought I ought to obey them so I was handcuffed, thrown into a paddywagon, taken to jail and put into the "tank" with a motley bunch of criminals. An old wino was passed out on one of the benches. I remembered that Jesus had said these signs shall follow them that believe, "In my name they shall cast out devils" (Mark 16:12). I laid my hands on a wino and commanded the devil, "Come out in the name of Jesus!" The wino was startled and jumped to his feet.

Turning around, I warned the prisoners that thiefs, drunkards, dope fiends and perverts would have their place in the LAKE of FIRE.

Soon the jailer rushed back and said, "Preacher, we are going to put you in solitary confinement."

I was slammed into a cell by myself. I remembered that Paul and Silas when they were put in jail prayed and sang praises unto God. So I fell to my knees and prayed, "God, get me out of this place," and I sang hymns. Later the jailer came back to photograph and fingerprint me. As we walked the corridor to the other end another prisoner thrust his hand through the bars and said, "Preacher, I want to shake hands with you."

Later, I was put back in my cell. I called to the man whose hand I had shook and asked, "Are you a Christian?"

He replied, "I am now. While you were praying and singing, I asked Jesus to save me."

This made my day! After four hours a friend arrived with money to bail me out.

The next day in court I thought the judge would surely be a reasonable man. I supposed that I would explain about the permit and he would dismiss the case. The arresting officer was there to witness against me. When I gave my side of the story, the haughty judge interrupted me asking, "What are you doing in Indianapolis anyway? There is plenty of sin in Terre Haute."

"You are right there, Your Honor," I answered, "But the Bible says 'Go into all the world and preach the gospel.' "

The judge said, "Why don't you go into one of the church buildings? That is what they are for."

I answered, "The buildings are places to come out of the weather and worship God in some comfort but Jesus said, 'Go into the highways and hedges, and compel them to come in that my house may be filled' " (Luke 14:23).

"Compel?" the ill-tempered judge snapped.

"This is what the Lord said."

"I have heard enough." (Evidently, the judge was being convicted by the Word). "Guilty! That will be a $25 fine."

"I want to appeal this decision."

The judge then stated the bail and had me incarcerated again until Max Lynch got the money together to bail me out. Meanwhile, I was able to lead another soul to the Lord.

Determined to get my message out on the streets of Indianapolis, I returned to the city controller to clear up the matter of a permit. But again he insisted it was not required. He did write a letter for me which stated a permit is not necessary to preach the Gospel on the streets of Indianapolis. I returned to Monument Circle and started preaching with my Bible in one hand and letter in the other. Within minutes a policeman approached me but I showed him the letter and he said, "Okay" and walked away.

I preached the Word unhindered for several days after that. I did not press my appeal since my right to preach had been established. It had cost me $25 but two souls had been saved from sin and hell.

Whether in city parking lots, at the street corners or on the campuses, calling sinners to repentance always creates NO SMALL STIR!

Mobbed at Kent State

At Kent State University the crowd became especially agitated and angry. Jim Gilles, a young evangelist, preached with me to a group of about 500. The more rowdy students threw forks and beer cans, spit at and mobbed us. Finally the police warned us that if the crowd did not quieten down, we would be arrested. They reasoned that it was easier to do something about us than the crowd. The enraged students became more violent. Suddenly we were both arrested. On the way to jail the officer apologized and said that he was not sure he had done the right thing and that he agreed with our message and liked the way we went about it.

The next day in court I appealed to the judge for an immediate dismissal of the case since the police admitted we had been arrested for our own safety. This time we had a fair judge who dropped the charges. That afternoon we travelled east toward the next university.

Two years later, in the fall of 1984, I returned to Kent State where the crowd reaction was considerably subdued. Dean John

Binder, who had courageously tired to protect me from irate students on my last visit, told me: "There is a conservative trend on the campus since the last time you were here. You may well have contributed to it."

Vindicated in New Orleans

At Tulane University a friend and attorney, Tom Elkins, accompanied me. Since Tulane is a private university, I preached on the public sidewalk in front of the campus. The campus police ordered me to stop but I informed them that I was within my rights. Next the city police came to the scene. They asked me to get in the car and Tom Elkins climbed in also. When Mr. Elkins tried to explain our rights, we were placed under arrest, driven downtown and ticketed.

The police did not bother to show up in court to testify against us so the judge dropped the case.

Mr. Elkins was quite upset over the violation of our constitutional rights and requested an apology from the police department. When they refused, he sued the City of New Orleans for $90,000. The case was settled out of court and we received a letter of apology and $1,000. The Apostle Paul appealed to his Roman citizenship when he was unlawfully bound. Thank God as Americans we still have freedom of speech but we must stand up for this freedom.

Triumphant Stand at Valdosta State

Our arrival on campus is often a shock and the campus authorities are usually inexperienced with handling such large crowd situations. We are very willing to explain our intentions and purposes to the authorities and conform to reasonable rules and regulations. The conflict arises when they absolutely deny our freedom of speech. If we insist on our rights and continue preaching often another campus is opened to public preaching. This is what happened when businessman and Bible teacher

Norval Hayes accompanied me to Valdosta State University in Georgia.

After a few minutes of preaching the chief of security ordered me to stop.

Whereupon I turned to 50 students and questioned, "Don't you have freedom of speech on this campus?"

The students yelled, "We sure do," and they began shouting at the chief, "Go back to your office, we want to hear the preacher. Go back to your office."

The crowd had doubled to 100 students when a uniformed policeman came to assist. By the time another policeman arrived there were 200 students. Then a dean came out and another dean. By this time we had a crowd of 250. When the vice president of the university arrived, I was in the middle of a crowd of 300 students, three policemen and two deans.

The vice president diplomatically said, "Reverend Smock, you come to my office and we will get this matter worked out privately."

I knew I had an advantage with 300 students continuously chanting, "Go back to your office. We want to hear the preacher."

I said to the vice president, "I am sorry, sir, but I don't feel led to do that."

"What do you mean you don't feel led?" asked the baffled administrator.

"I believe God wants me to stay out here with my class in 'Christianity 101, Basic Fundamentals of Christianity.' But if you agree to let me address the students, I will go in the cafeteria and talk with you for 15 minutes."

Reluctantly he agreed. In the cafeteria I shared my testimony and ministry with him.

He seemed impressed and said, "As I promised, you may speak now, but it will be a miracle if you can get a crowd after two o'clock on this campus on a Friday." (Evidently, many students customarily left early to go home for the weekend).

"No problem," I replied, "I believe in miracles."

Only a small group had waited around but as I started

preaching the crowd built up to a few hundred. I called on Norval Hayes.

God had spoken unto him and said, "These students don't know how to praise the Lord, show them how to praise." He fell to his knees and began to praise the Lord. The students were becoming convicted of sin.

I asked the crowd, "How many will pray that God will bring a revival to this campus?"

Those that volunteered joined hands with me. There must have been a hundred students in the prayer circle. Then I said, "Anyone who wants to get saved, pray after me." The court yard was filled with prayers of repentance toward God and faith toward Jesus Christ. Opening my eyes, I recognized the vice president in the crowd praying. Afterwords he congratulated us on our message and said that we were welcome on the campus anytime. He only requested that we let him know the next time we were coming.

Since this incident I have returned several times to minister at Valdosta State. The administration has faithfully cooperated. The vice president was promoted to the Board of Regents for the State University system in Georgia. The Word says: "For promotion cometh not from the east nor from the west, nor from the south; but God is the judge: He putteth down one and setteth up another" (Psalms 75:6, 7).

The Streets of Richmond, Indiana

Many who are converted through a street ministry initially have a zeal for outdoor witnessing. Yet once they gain respectability in the pulpit or pew they soon forget where they came from. The Lord has never allowed me to do this. Like Terre Haute, most American cities have a parking lot hangout similiar to the one where Clyde Swalls first witnessed to me. These cesspools of sin are filled with idle youth ripe for evangelism but largely ignored by timid Christians.

In August of 1983, Cindy and I went to Richmond, Indiana for a week. I was scheduled to speak in three churches. Friday night after service a large group from the congregation followed us out to a shopping center parking lot where we preached to the youth who were cruising the streets in revelry. Immediately we got the attention of several hundred bored juveniles who soon became very excited and angry. The police watched for awhile then one of them told me there was a problem. I informed him that there sure was a big problem with these drunken, doped, rock 'n rolled and sex-crazed delinquents roaming the streets but we were part of the SOLUTION. Though the police and community are satisfied to maintain a high level of tolerance for the wanton youth, God will not tolerate sin and neither should Christians!

Finally the police ordered us to go over to the other side of the parking lot and if the youth followed us we could continue preaching. I agreed, moved a block away and began speaking. Within 15 minutes the crowd followed us and the police left the scene. God's people were now in control of the situation. The next night Christians from other churches met with us out in the lot for another stirring time of evangelism.

I was very impressed with the enthusiastic support we received from the Richmond Christians, none of whom had seen or done any witnessing in this manner. Before I left town a number of them made a commitment to continue the street work. After leaving we received several letters from Richmond informing us that the ministry was still going on. Sinners had repented and backsliders had come back to the Lord!

TOO LONG Christians have been ministering one to another in the confines of a church building while their children are reveling in the streets, cruising top speed toward HELL. WAKE UP CHRISTIANS! Get stirred in your spirit. Drive out the devil. Cry out against SIN. Get activated. Be bold and courageous. God is sick of this mealy-mouthed, rubber-necked, chicken-hearted, banana-backed, jelly-bellied, limp wristed, weak-kneed and flat-footed so-called Christianity. Rise up against evil and let us go forth to BATTLE, tearing down Satan's strongholds by calling people to righteousness and holiness.

Sister Cindy Arrested at Chico State

To take stands like this always means that we run the risk of being arrested. That is what happened to Sister Cindy in March of 1984 at Chico State University in Northern California.

Our first day at Chico State, "Holy Hubert" Lindsey and Evangelist and Mrs. George Davis joined us for an afternoon of tagteam preaching. We took turns warning and exhorting crowds of several hundred until late that afternoon.

That night we held a special meeting in a local church. Nine Chico State students came to the service eager to hear more. We were anticipating even greater campus meetings the next day — ignorant of the forces at work to hinder our vital mission.

A student who leads a so-called Christian campus fellowship phoned me the next morning. This wolf in sheep's clothing said his group had scheduled the "free speech" area for the purpose of keeping us off campus. They claimed our method and message lacked love. True, we do not have the humanistic, lawless, tongue-love of this perverted generation. We do have the message of the love of God that leads a man to forsake selfishness, obey God and even love his enemies. Our love for the students compelled us to return to the "free speech" area and exercise our First Amendment rights.

The campus security, also biased against our straight-forward message, forced us off campus with the threat of arrest. It was frustrating to leave a crowd of 100 students who obviously wanted to hear us. Therefore, we decided to preach from the city sidewalk on the edge of campus.

Within minutes city police sped to the scene and informed Cindy they had a complaint against her. She was ordered to stop preaching immediately or move further from campus. At this point Cindy felt she had retreated far enough. Since she refused to move she was handcuffed, placed in the squad car, booked, fingerprinted and thrown in jail. Cindy preached to everyone in the police station before Brother Davis bailed her out for $500 two hours later. They were glad to see her leave! God provided us with a wise Christian lawyer who handled the case — free of charge. Although the judge found her guilty, he set aside the penalty and our bail was refunded.

Many criticize preachers for defying the authorities, but Charles Spurgeon, in his Lectures to My Students, said:

> "I am somewhat pleased when I occasionally hear of a brother's being locked up by police, for it does him good, and it does the people good also. It is a fine sight to see the minister of the gospel marched off by the servant of the law! It excites sympathy for him, and the next step is sympathy for his message. Many who felt no interest in him before are eager to hear him when he is ordered to leave off, and still more so when he is taken to the station. The vilest of mankind respect a man who gets into trouble in order to do them good, and if they see unfair opposition excited they grow quite zealous in the man's defense.

After Cindy was apprehended I moved to a nearby city park to continue the message. I lost many of the college crowd but was able to draw a group of junior high and high school students. That night eight teenage punk-rockers came to the church with the father of one of the girls, a local obstetrician. At the end of the service I allowed time for a question-and-answer period. To the shock of church members, the youth were very blunt about their unbelief, immorality and drug use. The evening was as beneficial to the church people as to the young revelers. Conservative pew warmers need to find out what is threatening this nation and take a stand while there's something left to stand for!

We later received a letter from a David Knehne in Chico who has chosen to take such a stand:

> Dear Brother Jed and Cindy,
>   I am very thankful to God for your ministry. I wish you could have spent more time in Chico and especially on campus. I believed that meeting you was divinely appointed. You have really challenged me and set my heart

burning to know God in a deeper way . . . You were like a breath of fresh air in a smoke-filled room . . .

Oh, that I could throw my life away, that others might know Christ. I too pray that I will be able to lay down my life and follow the path that Jesus walked to the cross, not caring what men think but fearing God only . . .

In a second letter Brother Dave reported that he and a friend had been witnessing in the Chico city park to the youth hanging out in revelry every Saturday night!

If we had never resisted the authorities there are dozens of campuses that would be closed to our ministry and other outdoor preachers. The Bible is filled with examples of men who chose to obey God rather than governments: Daniel, Jeremiah and the apostles are only a few.

If the apostles had stopped preaching when they were told, we would not have a church today. We must take a stand even if it means going to jail, yea, even if it means laying down one's life. We must take the Gospel to the public places. The apostles did not invite people to church in the first century — the church came to the people. This is the Bible way of spreading the word. Some have called this ministry radical Christianity.

*The position that we occupy
is that the Christian faith is the
perfection of human reason.
— Noah Porter, President
of Yale College, 1878*

10

THE UNIVERSITIES FROM CHRIST TO DARWIN ... AND BEYOND

"Why do you preach on college campuses everyday? Are we the only sinners?" a student once asked.

"No, but tomorrow you may be the most INFLUENTIAL sinners unless I can persuade you to become INFLUENTIAL saints!" I reply.

The center of influence in Jesus' day was the synagogue. That is where you found our Lord much of the time. I am convinced that if the Son of God had come to the United States in the twentieth century, rather than Israel in the first century, he would have gone to the campuses. THE UNIVERSITIES CONTROL THE MIND OF AMERICA.

As go the campuses so goes the nation. The college students are tomorrow's politicians, lawyers, doctors, educators, bureaucrats, journalists, businessmen and corporation leaders. If there is going to be a national awakening, this is the stratum of society that must be reached. The hippie radical movement started at

Berkeley and spread like wildfire to the other campuses. The same could happen today with a movement of the Spirit of God among the students.

Collegians are at a crucial age. During these years they are making choices that will determine the direction of their lives. They are away from home for the first time. They are idealistic — still questioning and looking for answers to the issues of life. Their hearts are relatively tender. However, after graduation comes a career, marriage or "alternate life-style." Graduates soon settle into life's daily routines and struggles. Their hearts grow indifferent and callous. After leaving school the probability of their ever converting diminishes considerably.

The universities are communities within themselves. Some have over 50,000 students, and also the professors, administrators and staff. Yet, local churches and campus ministries have failed miserably to reach them. It will be a terrible day at judgment when believers realize that the blood of multitudes of college students will be on their hands because they did not "rise up for God against the evildoers, and stand with him against the workers of iniquity." They have refused to warn the wicked to turn from their wickedness and live.

The Failure of the Church World

The local churches are family-oriented institutions and, therefore, the typical pastor does not include the students in his vision. He does not see how they can be much help in building a great church. Many pastors are intimidated by students, wrongly considering them to be intellectuals. Some feel they don't have the education or the knowledge to deal with them.

The churches are spending millions of dollars to take the Gospel to the nations of the world but they are ignoring the thousands of foreign students in their own back yards. On campuses we regularly preach to students from the four corners of the earth. Many who hear us are from nations that are virtually closed to missionaries.

In 1983 we met a man at the University of Louisville. He was from Saudi Arabia and had been in America for only three weeks. Although raised a Moslem, he said he desired to read the Bible and become a Christian. But he feared that if he converted he would be killed when he returned home. After instructing him in the Word we introduced the young Arab to a believer who invited him to a Bible study.

A group of Iranian Moslem students at the University of Illinois told Brother Lynch and me that we are very well known in their country. Iranians on campuses all over the United States have heard us and returned to their own nation to talk of our preaching.

Some campus ministries are weak and socially oriented. They have built "Christian centers" with pool and ping pong tables that emphasize recreation and socialization, not the Gospel and worship. The ranks of these ministries are filled with individuals who are vexed and intimidated by the filthy conduct of the students. They have compromised with the world to the point that they have stripped themselves of any power with God or man. Campus "Christians" are preoccupied with humanistic studies and their social lives. These "evangelicals," with their lukewarm version of Christianity and ignorance of biblical doctrine and sound theology, are the GREATEST HINDRANCE to the spread of the Gospel today.

The liberals have united to build centers that usually go under the banner of the United Campus Ministry. They often are hotbeds of homosexuals, lesbians, socialists, women libbers, abortionists and their sympathizers. We are a thorn in the flesh to these ecumenicals who view us with ridicule and contempt. Even though they bear the name of Christ, the liberals will go to great lengths to disassociate themselves from us.

At a Big Ten university a local church invited me to speak for three evening services. The meetings were scheduled at the Wesley Foundation, an ecumenical building just off campus. After we advertised the services in the school newspaper, the foundation called the church pastor on the carpet. When he defended my Gospel preaching, a Wesley Foundation minister cursed: "*!#!**!#, I don't believe what he is preaching is the

Gospel!" He also wrote a letter to the editor of the newspaper denouncing my preaching. This ecumenicalist had suddenly become unecumenical.

The Campus Pulpit

Before the era of shopping malls the downtown square was an ideal place for reaching people. Preachers could gather great crowds by preaching in towns and cities throughout America. Today, however, the downtowns are deserted and the streets and sidewalks of major cities are too congested with automobiles and pedestrians in a hurry to do business. City ordinances often unconstitutionally prohibit street preaching without a permit, which is often difficult to obtain.

The campuses are a more secluded environment which have lawns, malls and patios providing natural places for students to gather between classes. There is no street and traffic noise to hinder the message from being heard. Most universities have a free speech policy and tradition. Actually, it would be more accurate to call us campus preachers rather than street preachers.

Street ministers have the disadvantage of attempting to witness to people that are often under the influence of alcohol or drugs. Their minds are preoccupied with the immediate satisfactions of the lusts of the flesh.

We preach during the day when the students are still sober. They have been exercising their intellects in the classrooms and are often anxious to engage in discussion. We introduce contemporary issues in a biblical context. We present the opposite of what they have heard in the humanistic classrooms. Argument and debate result and it draws a larger crowd. Sparks fly for awhile but when the students calm down we are able to teach effectively. This is important since few students have heard the biblical doctrines accurately presented and defended. It has not always been this way.

Consider the Paths of Our Fathers

In the stone gateway to Ohio University, founded in 1804, is engraved this quotation from the Congressional Ordinance of 1787: "Religion, morality and knowledge being necessary to good government and the happiness of mankind, schools and the means of education shall forever be encouraged." Obviously, our Founding Fathers never intended to separate religion and morality from education. They recognized that religion, morality and knowledge were the fundamentals of education, good government and a happy people.

In fact, America's most prestigious universities, Harvard, William and Mary, Yale and Princeton were founded to prepare men for the clergy. The Bible was the chief text and theology was the main course of study. The charter of William and Mary, written in 1693, states the college was founded "to the end that the church of Virginia may be furnished with a seminary of ministers of the gospel, and that the youth may be piously educated in good letters and manners, and that the Christian faith may be propagated among the Western Indians, to the glory of Almighty God."

In colonial America religion was the major influence on student life. Each college required daily chapel and prayer, Sunday church attendance and divinity studies. Student conduct was closely regulated according to the moral precepts of Christianity. For example, the first code of Harvard laws in 1646 provided the following: "Everyone shall consider the main end of his life and studies, to know God and Jesus Christ which is eternal life. Seeing the Lord giveth wisdom, everyone shall seriously, by prayer in secret, seek wisdom of Him. Everyone shall so exercise himself in reading the scriptures twice a day that they may be ready to give an account of their proficiency therein . . ."

This emphasis was not limited to the colleges founded by the church denominations. The 1785 charter of the University of Georgia said that in order to promote national prosperity one of the institution's first objectives would be to encourage and support the principles of Christianity and morality and to provide the instruction that would mold the students to the love of virtue and good order. To accomplish this, the ninth law of the charter required that all professors and administrators be of the Christian religion, and take a public oath of allegiance and fidelity.

Through the nineteenth century practically all institutions of higher learning had compulsory daily chapel services for faculty and students.

"We all attended chapel in those days (1890), and took turns in conducting the exercises; each took his turn in reading an appropriate selection from the Bible and elucidating its religious and ethical meaning," said Dr. Barton W. Everman of Indiana State University.

Even so, there was a constant battle throughout the nineteenth century between the religious and the secular sectors on campuses. Sporadic revivals helped Christianity maintain eminence during this time. However, in the twentieth century the majority of colleges began to develop a vast extra-curricular program making it difficult for religious organizations to compete successfully with intercollegiate athletics, the social programs of fraternities and sororities and other secular student groups. Finally, in the 1920s the state universities wielded the death blow to organized religion by making chapel attendance optional. Consequently, by the end of the 1930s chapel instruction virtually died and today is nonexistent. Theology, once considered the queen of the sciences, lost academic respectability.

Although the state universities led the way in secularism, the church-founded institutions were not far behind in ousting Christianity. Today I find more believers on the state campuses than at Harvard, Yale, Princeton, Oberlin and other church-related institutions.

The Spirit of Finney Returns

Charles Finney, America's greatest theologian and evangelist, was president of Oberlin College in Ohio during the mid-nineteenth century. I desired to preach at Oberlin because it had been a great evangelical institution and the heart of the revivals of that period. In the Spring of 1978 the Lord directed me to go there.

After I preached only five minutes campus security stopped me and suggested I get permission from the administration to continue.

I was directed to the chaplain's office. He sat at his desk wearing a T-shirt, bermuda shorts and shower tongs and smoking a cigarette. He constantly made reference to God in the female gender. Reluctantly he decided, "She (meaning God to him) would not mind if I spoke at Oberlin."

At sometime during the day almost every student in the college must have listened. However, not one would acknowledge the Bible to be the Word of God. After seven and a half hours, I closed the meeting. Later the chaplain said to me, "We have never had anything like this at Oberlin. I listened to you all afternoon. I will have to admit that you really had something going out there today. Of course, I don't agree with your theology at all."

Not only did the chaplain and the whole campus oppose me, but they showed there gross ignorance of Oberlin's evangelical and revival heritage and Charles Finney's ministry and theology. To them Finney is just the name of the chapel where they hold their rock concerts. Regretably, Oberlin is typical of the once Christian colleges that have long since rejected the paths and teachings of their Fathers.

They Hated Knowledge

"When they knew God, they glorified Him not as God, neither were they thankful; but became vain in their imaginations, and their foolish heart was darkened. Professing themselves to be wise, they became fools. Who CHANGED THE TRUTH OF GOD INTO A LIE, and worshipped and served

the creature more than the Creator, who is blessed forever"
(Romans 1:21, 22-25).

The universities have exchanged the truth of God our Creator for the lies of Charles Darwin and the evolutionists!

They have exchanged the truth of Jesus Christ our Redeemer for the lies of Marx and Engles who would enslave man!

They have exchanged the truth of God, our great teacher, for the lies of John Dewey, Sigmund Freud and many other "foolosophers!"

They have exchanged the truth of Christian theology for the vain imaginations of the secular humanists.

Christian theology is the thoughts and principles of God. Humanism is the thoughts and principles of man. Theology is knowledge centered on the Creator. Humanism is knowledge centered on the creature. According to Webster's New Collegiate Dictionary, knowledge "is a clear perception of the truth." It is impossible for man to have a clear understanding of truth without sound theology. Therefore, a rejection of theology is in effect a rejection of knowledge. The Word says: "And unto man God said, 'Behold the fear of the Lord, that is wisdom; and to depart from evil is understanding' " (Job 28:28).

The University of Minnesota was founded in 1851. The following inscription is engraved in stone on the front of Northrop Memorial Auditorium: "The University of Minnesota founded in faith that men are enobled by understanding, dedicated to the advancement of learning and the search for the truth, devoted to instruction of the youth and the welfare of the state." This statement of purpose is pretentious and secular in comparison to the godly and ethical emphasis at the establishment of Ohio University, the University of Georgia and the colonial colleges.

The University of Minnesota is searching for the truth. The Bible speaks of men "ever learning but never able to come to a knowledge of the truth" (II Timothy 3:7). Thousands of Minnesota students pass Northrop Auditorium each day going to classes seeking after knowledge.

Annually, since 1974, I have stood in front of the auditorium with Bible raised and cried out to the passing students, "I've found it. I found it. I found it. Stop searching, I FOUND IT," I cry out.

Soon a crowd gathers, wondering what I had found.

"I found the TRUTH!"

"Jesus said, 'I am the Truth.' He is the source of truth for all who diligently seek it," I tell them.

University of Minnesota students and professors have supposedly been searching for the truth for about 150 years. But they rejected the teacher of truth and, as the angel said to Mary, they blindly sought the living among the dead. Their search for truth among the lies proved futile, so today many have come to the conclusion that there is no truth.

As the religious teaching waned throughout the twentieth century, universities still attempted to enforce moral behavior with restrictive rules and regulations, especially on the women. For example, into the mid-sixties dorm curfews were placed on the girls and visitation of the opposite sex in private rooms was strictly forbidden. But the attempt to promote virtue was doomed to failure because the foundation of morality — the Christian religion — had been rejected. It is impossible to establish Christian ethics in the heart of man without Jesus Christ. Without the truths and promises of Christianity, the motives and incentives for being moral are lost.

Rat Lab

As a freshman at Indiana University in 1960 I was on a liberal arts curriculum and we were required to take five hours of psychology. I will never forget my first day in Psychology 101 lab. Each member of the class was assigned a white rat in a cage with a bag of rat food.

"Is this what higher education is all about, studying the behavior of rats?" I thought to myself.

We made stimulus-response-type experiments through feeding and withholding food from the rats and observing their behavior. After a few days in class I figured out what it was all about. My professor came from the behaviorist school of psychology. His mentor was B.F. Skinner who denied man is a free moral agent. The behaviorists believe that man is conditioned to act in a certain manner by his environment. FROM OUR STUDY OF RATS WE WERE TO DRAW CONCLUSIONS ABOUT NORMAL HUMAN BEHAVIOR.

Evolution

Behaviorism is an outgrowth of evolution. Both behaviorists and evolutionists fail to recognize the distinction of man from the animal kingdom. Animals are primarily creatures of instinct, whereas men are free moral agents. Althought man has instincts, he is not to let them govern him. God designed man to be governed by moral law.

Students had been told they were animals for so long that finally, in the late 1960s, they began to look and act like animals. Today many college students have no more morals than cockroaches.

When I was preaching at the University of Iowa a graduate student in biology argued evolution versus creation with me all afternoon. Each time he raised his hand to make a comment or ask a question, I called him animal. Finally, late in the afternoon, he said,

"You better not call me animal again. I'm getting tired of it!"

"Ahaa!" I cried, "You have believed evolution with your head but your heart tells you that you are more than an animal."

The student was rightfully offended when I called him an animal, because something deep down inside told him he was more than beast. Men may argue vociferously to defend evolution but when you begin to treat them like animals they will quickly object.

Logically, it must be concluded if God created man in his image, then man is responsible to God. But since man does not want to be responsible to God, he has rejected the knowledge of God and substituted it for the vain imaginations of the evolutionists, behaviorists and other schools of thought.

Paul accused the Athenian intellectuals of spending their "time in nothing else, but to either tell, or hear some new thing" (Acts 17:21). So it is with the so-called intellectuals on the campuses. Popular philosophies and ideas come in and out of vogue like the length of women's skirts.

Humanistic Psychology

In 1970 I was doing post-graduate work at Indiana State University and taking courses in counseling and psychology. By this time behaviorism seemed on the wane and it had been replaced by humanistic psychology. The behaviorist had studied animals to draw conclusions about human behavior but now the practice was to observe other human beings in the laboratory of a therapy group session. The idea was for individuals to set aside social restraints and "let go" in order to vent their true feelings and thoughts. I soon got into the swing of things and suggested that we have a group orgy. The professor who led the group said, "Jed, we are just not ready to handle that YET."

Theology

So the behaviorists study animals to learn normal human behavior and humanistic psychologists study other humans; but what does the Christian study? He studies theology which is the science of God. The Christian knows that man is made in the image of God. Therefore, he studies the character and attributes of God. He studies God's holiness, love, mercy, justice, wisdom, etc. because he knows that man is supposed to be God-like in character. The Christian knows that sin, hatred, malice, impatience, injustice, etc. are contrary to man's nature because these things result in death.

"The position which we occupy is that the Christian faith is the perfection of human reason; that supernatural and historical Christianity is the only Christianity which is worth defending or which is capable of being defended on the grounds of reason or history; and that such Christianity, when interpreted by enlightened judgment, as to its truths and precepts, is not only friendly to the highest forms of culture, but is an essential condition of the same," said Noah Porter, the President of Yale College, in 1878.

Can a man take fire in his bosom,
and his clothes not be burned?
Proverbs 6:27

11

SEX, BOOZE, DRUGS
AND ROCK 'N ROLL

"FOR A WHORE IS A DEEP DITCH and a strange
woman is a narrow pit. She lieth in wait as for a prey, and
increaseth the transgressions among men!" (Proverbs 23:27,
28).

In my early campus ministry I cautioned the girls to beware of
the immoral men but in later years I saw an increasing need to
also warn the men about lewd women. This admonition is
prominent in the scriptures. The verse above is just one of the
many examples in the book of Proverbs that cautions men about
the tragic results of involvement with seductive women.

The Parable of the Five Dormies

Proverbs 7 gives a graphic description of a man falling prey to
a whorish woman. Putting this theme in a contemporary setting,
I often relate to the students the Parable of the FIVE DORMIES:

When these five young men were in high school they could not wait to get to the university because they had heard how so many of the dorms were hotbeds of fornication and how so many of these dorm girls were "hot to trot."

The first dormie was Brian. He seemed to be an intelligent young man. He had graduated top of his high school class, was number one in the state debate team and was going to be a doctor. He was from a poor family but had received a full-paid scholarship. Brian wanted to put his studies first but, like a lot of young men, he also wanted to get involved with the promiscuous women. His first night in the dorm he met LUSTFUL LISA. He said, "Lisa, how 'bout if we go out to eat and take in a movie?"

She said, "Oh, Brian, you must be a freshman; we don't do things like that here at the university — FIRST we go to bed and see how much we have in common . . ."

Within 30 minutes Brian and Lustful Lisa were in bed fornicating. Then Brian patted himself on the back and thought, "I've got a pretty good thing here."

But there was one problem; Lustful Lisa like to have sex ALL the time. She got Brian to skip his classes and, whenever he would come home to study, there she'd be in his dorm room just waiting to lure him into bed. Since Brian attended so few classes and had so little time to study, he flunked out his very first semester. He lost his scholarship and could not go back to school. Today, Brian is working at McDONALDS.

The second dormie was Fred. He was studying agriculture and going to be a farmer. Fred was from a nice rural town in Iowa. He was in love and engaged to marry a young virgin back home. But he thought as long as he was at the university, he might as well, "sow his wild oats," and get involved with the promiscuous women. His first week in the dorm, Fred met SEXY SARAH. He told Sarah she was pretty and five minutes later he had her pants off. Fred patted himself on the back and thought, "I've got a pretty good thing here." But there was one problem: lots of men had told Sexy Sarah she was pretty and lots of men had gotten her pants off— Sexy Sarah was a carrier of VD! Not only was it VD, it was the incurable HERPES II! Within a couple of weeks some ugly red sores appeared on Fred's private parts. Of course, he had to tell his fiance' back home . . . she immediately broke off the engagement! Fred was so hurt, he was so broken-hearted, that he went out and committed suicide.

The third dormie was Jerry: Jerry thought he was a real jock. He was a football player. But Jerry wasn't just any football player. Even though he was a freshman, Jerry was already playing first string and the pro scouts already had their eyes on him. Yet, like a lot of college boys, Jerry wanted to get involved with the lewd women. His first week in the football dorm Jerry met DAIQUIRI DONNA. Daiquiri Donna like to fornicate but there was one thing she liked better than her fornication, her strawberry and banana daiquiries. Jerry thought, "What the heck, I'll buy her a few daiquiries; it's worth it to get her into bed." But Jerry made the mistake of drinking daiquiries with her. First it was once a week, then twice a week, then almost every opportunity they had Jerry and Donna were drinking and fornicating. By the time spring football practice came around, Jerry had begun to crave alcohol. In the fall Jerry made the mistake of going to practice under the influence of alcohol. The coach warned him but Jerry could not help himself; he had to have those daiquiries, he had to have those daiquires, HE HAD TO HAVE THOSE DAIQUIRIES! Finally Jerry went to a game under the influence of alcohol; it was the last straw — the coach kicked him off the team — his whole career went down the drain, thanks to the influence of a whorish woman!

The fourth dormie was Larry. Larry, who also seemed to

be an intelligent young man, was studying to be a lawyer. But he lacked wisdom and wanted to get involved with the promiscuous women. Larry's first week in the dorm he met **POTHEAD PAULA**. Pothead Paula was willing to fornicate but she felt guilty about all her immorality. To escape her guilt, she always had to get high on marijuana. Larry made the mistake of getting high with her. Before long they were using speed, then Quaaludes, then cocaine . . . After drawing many lines they moved on to LSD. To support their habits Larry and Pothead Paula had to start dealing in drugs. One day they were going to make a big deal; all the drugs were stashed in Paula's dormroom. Paula went up to Larry and started kissing him passionately right on the lips. Within a few seconds they were in bed together. Suddenly, a knock came to the door; BANG, BANG, BANG . . . It was the POLICE; Larry and Pothead Paula got busted. So instead of becoming a lawyer, Larry had to hire a lawyer; today he's serving 10 to 15 years in the penitentiary.

The fifth and final dormie was Horny Harry. Horny Harry was not as handsome as the other four, so he had to take whatever he could get. Finally, after three weeks in the dorm, Horny Harry met **ROCK 'N ROLL RHONDA**. Rhonda like to fornicate but there was one thing she liked better than her fornication: her Rock 'n Roll music. She liked to listen to The Who, to Led Zeppelin, Pink Floyd, the Grateful Dead, Black Sabbath, Deep Purple, Rush, AC/DC, The Sex Pistols, and she just loved, loved, loved that pervert **MICK JAGGER**. Rock 'n Rolling Rhonda liked to go to rock concerts and she would get Horny Harry to go with her. She always had to stand right down in front. One night the music was so loud that it busted one of Harry's eardrums. He still had one left. Whenever Horny Harry and Rock 'n Rolling Rhonda were commiting fornication she always had to have that rock music just blaring. These rock 'n roll demons entered Harry and they began to speak to him . . . Do you know what they said? "Harry, you're a queer, Harry, you lust after men, Harry, you're a HO-MO-SEX-U-AL!" So Harry dropped out of school and today he's cruising in San Francisco. By now poor Harry probably has AIDS disease.

There you have it folks, five men down the drain thanks to five whorish women.

Brazen Women

Isaiah sharply rebuked the women of his day for their shameless, brazen behavior and vain dress. He said, "Therefore the Lord will smite with a scab the heads of the daughters of Zion and the Lord will lay bare their secret parts" (Isaiah 3:17).

Many of the mastectomies performed today may be a result of God's judgment on women for using their breasts as mere sex objects and not desiring to have a baby or much less nurse one. Most college girls would rather slurp beer than nurse a baby. Many hysterectomies may be a consequence of women illicitly flaunting their private parts instead of using them for their primary design of conception. Since many use birth control, and others are murdering their own babies, God is making them disgracefully barren.

The Bible says, "Women adorn themselves in modest apparel, with shamefacedness and sobriety; not with braided hair, or gold, or pearls, or costly array; but (which becometh women professing Godliness) with good works" (I Timothy 2:9,10).

At the University of Texas a student asked, "Just what is modest apparel?"

I pointed out a girl whose skirt was covering her knees and said, "She is dressed modestly." But to let me and everyone else know she was not modest she lifted her skirt and showed everything.

I responded, "That proves one can't judge by appearance, she looks modest, but obviously she is not."

"Try again Brother Jed, try again," someone shouted.

I pointed to another girl similarly dressed. She blushed and tried to hide in the crowd.

"There is a girl who not only is dressed modestly, but evidently she is modest. When is the last time you saw one of these college girls blush?"

"Were they ashamed when they had committed abomination? Nay, they were not ashamed, neither could they blush. . . Therefore, at the time I visit they shall be cast down," saith the Lord (Jeremiah 6:15).

Many girls walk around campus braless and, on numerous occasions to the delight of the boys, they have flashed their bare breasts toward me. No wonder there are so many rapes on college campuses. Those girls walking and jogging around campus with their shorts so short that their buttocks hang out are just asking for it. They might as well have a sign on their back saying, "Rape me, rape me, rape me."

Regretably, many girls in their shorts and halter tops even claim to be Christians. When they change their shorts, they put on their tight designer jeans. What are designer jeans designed for? Obviously for sex appeal. No woman professing godliness would want to wear clothing that accentuates the curves of her body. When a man of God delivers this message many of the women get very contentious. They don't want a preacher telling them how they should dress, yet they will let some limp-wrist, fairy, clothing designer in New York or Paris determine their dress code.

Unisex

Deuteronomy 22:5 gives some important guidelines on dress! "The woman shall not wear that which pertaineth to a man, neither shall a man put on a woman's garment: for all that do so are an abomination unto the Lord thy God." This is a clear warning against the contemporary unisex look.

God planned different roles for men and women. He made them Adam and Eve, not Adam and Steve. They are different and their inequalities are to complement one another. Therefore, men and women are to talk, walk, look and dress differently. The unisex look leads of confusion which often results in perversion. When a generation of mothers puts on the trousers and cropped their hair, it paved the way for the long-haired hippies and Tiny Tims of the 60s right through to the skirt-wearing Boy Georges and feminine-voiced Michael Jacksons of the 80s.

The New Testament reinforces the necessity of the distinction of the sexes: "Doth not even nature itself teach you, that if a man have long hair, it is a shame to him? But if a woman have long hair, it is a glory to her: for her hair is given her for a covering" (I Corinthians 11:14,15).

Only a generation ago schools and colleges had dress codes but, since the barriers have been let down, anything goes including occasional streakers. Parents, professors and ministers are silent on this matter — they either condone it or are afraid to speak out for fear of "turning people off." Actually, many of the professors and some of the so-called campus ministers dress as lewdly as the students.

Many argue it does not matter what you wear. However, say something critical about their attire and, by their vehement response, one will discover that dress IS one of their primary considerations.

One of the student's favorite scriptures is that "man looketh on the outward appearance, but God looketh on the heart." This is precisely the point. Since it is man's nature to be stimulated by exposed flesh, the body must be covered properly. Christians are ambassadors for Christ. We represent the Kingdom of God. Therefore, I always want to look my best. Hence, when preaching I dress professionally. In campus society it is fashionable to **dress down. Most students and many immature professors make an effort to be slovenly.** When young men and women professing to represent Jesus Christ conform to the lowly vogue of this generation they rob themselves of their dignity and disgrace the Kingdom of God. Our bodies are the temples of the Holy Spirit. They should be attired in a manner befitting to the Holy One who dwells in us and not dressed as an indolent sluggard.

It was two months after my conversion that I came to these conclusions. I will always remember the Sunday morning I walked into Rosedale Assembly of God with a short haircut, clean shaven and wearing a coat and tie. The congregation had never seen me in anything but my hippie attire and they thought I was a visitor!

My change on the outside was evidence to man that my change on the inside had been genuine. Likewise the lewd dress of contemporary society is evidence of the complete breakdown of the sexual morals of this generation.

Fornication

"What's wrong if I sleep with my boyfriend? He loves me!" a student asked.

"Oh, woman," I replied, "don't tell me you have fallen for one of the oldest lines in the book. He doesn't love you. If he loved you, he would want to marry you before he had intimate relations with you. The Bible says, 'Marriage is honourable in all, and the bed undefiled: but whoremongers and adulterers God will judge' " (Hebrews 13:4).

A whore is a woman who engages in unlawful sexual intercourse. A whoremonger is one who fornicates with whores. In God's sight a woman fornicator is a whore, whether she sells her body or gives it away. Sexual expression outside of marriage is forbidden by God's law. Fornication is illicit sexual intercourse on the part of an unmarried person. Adultery is sexual intercourse between a married person and anyone other than the lawful spouse. Personally, I have more respect for the professional prostitute than the girl that gives it away. At least the professionals put some value on their bodies.

The college campuses are becoming so wicked that I don't see how a professional whore could make a living in a college town, since there are so many strumpets, slatterns and trollops in the dorms giving it away. In addition there are more hussies, tarts and vixens in the sorority houses.

One day when I was warning the students about the evils of sexual sin, and blessings of sexual purity, a boy challenged me asking, "Would you buy a car without test driving it?"

Quickly, I replied, "But if I find out its got mileage on it, I won't buy it. I want a new car, you may have the used car."

"Know ye not that your bodies are the members of Christ? Shall I then take the members of Christ, and make them the members of a harlot? God forbid" (I Corinthians 6:15).

"Flee fornication" (I Corinthians 6:18).

God has given us the sexual appetite. It is what psychologists call the sexual drive. I prefer not to use the Freudian term "drive" because that implies that sex is a compulsion or obsession. We are not to be driven by sex. We are to be led of the Holy Spirit. The only legitimate expression of our sexual appetite is in the sanctity of holy matrimony. It is perversion for the mind to be preoccupied with lustful thoughts. The advertiser's emphasis on sexual appeal proves that the American mind is fixed on lust. But God intended our thoughts to be concentrated on benevolence toward him and our fellow man.

Jesus said, "That whosoever looketh on a woman to lust after her hath committed adultery with her already in his heart" (Matthew 5:28).

Sodomy

Lust is unlawful sexual intentions. Masturbation is one of the first expressions of lust. Your masturbator of today is very likely to be your homosexual of tomorrow. Your homosexual of tomorrow could be your psychology professor of the next day. In fact, universities are graduating more queers than Ph.Ds.

Homosexuality has become accepted on the university campuses as an "alternate life-style." But the Holy God of the universe still calls it an abomination, unnatural, vile and the result of a reprobate mind.

"If a man also lieth with mankind as with a woman, both of them have committed an abomination and they shall surely be put to death" (Leviticus 20:13).

Romans 1:25 warns that when a man exchanges the truth of God for a lie he is a candidate for sodomy. This is exactly what has happened in the state education system. The truth of God's Word has been exchanged for the lies of evolutionists, humanists, socialists and perverts. Anyone who believes these lies opens himself to uncleanness and inordinate affections. We warn of these dangers and cry out against homosexuality every day. It's not unusual for students to admit before the whole crowd that they are "Gay" and proud of it.

Many people laugh at this sin and most Christians ignore it — hoping it will go away. Lot had the same attitude and he was vexed to the point of offering his own virgin daughters to a gang of Sodomites. Another time the nation of Israel ignored this sin in their midst until a woman was raped all night to the point of death by a group of angry homosexuals (Judges 19).

For the glory of God, our nation and our posterity we are compelled to attack this issue head-on. At the University of Wisconsin in the fall of 1983 we held two anti-homosexual seminars which turned the campus upside down. We advertised the meeting with a pink flyer promising to give Bible answers to the following questions:

1. Why do homosexuals contact AIDS disease?
2. Are people born homosexuals?
3. Why do people become homosexuals?
4. What are the characteristics of a homosexual?
5. What should you do if you find out your roommate is a homosexual?
6. What should you do if you think you are a homosexual?
7. Can a homosexual be happy?
8. Does God hate homosexuals?
9. What happens to homosexuals when they die?

Sodomite men packed into the front rows of the meeting room flaunting their sin without shame. Some even kissed on the lips. I projected the Bible verses on a large screen so they could read God's condemnation of such abominable practices.

The second night a Christian man, Dewayne W., who had been a homosexual for 22 years and involved in the "Gay Rights Movement" in San Francisco, gave a powerful testimony and message. About 40 sodomites heard Brother Dewayne give a firsthand account of the tragic, miserable and anything but "Gay" life-style. He boldly proclaimed that JESUS had made him a new creation and a normal man and would do the same for them. Some mocked, some cursed and some listened with serious expressions of conviction.

The homosexual protests coupled with the complaints of the liberal campus ministries provoked an administrator to say, "Your student group has generated more controversy in this community than any organization on campus ever has!"

He admitted that some of the groups that had fought the hardest to be recognized by the university were striving to remove us from campus. Today the homosexuals do not receive any persecution from university authorities. In fact, the sodomites are given university funds to advertise their gay-lesbian dances held in the student union.

Society may try to pass this behavior off as normal but nature proclaims "It is not!" The Bible says: "And likewise also the men, leaving the natural use of the woman, burned in their lust one toward another; men with men working that which is unseemly, and receiving in themselves that recompence of their error which was meet" (Romans 1:27).

In other words they got what they deserved. The cursed AIDS disease is a natural consequence of such perverted behavior. It is nature's severe way of telling people they are doing things for which they were never designed. The fact that innocent babies have suffered with AIDS disease should tell us that we cannot sit back and ignore such sins against God and nature. If we do, all will suffer. When God brought judgment on Israel, the righteous Jeremiah was carried captive with the guilty. The actions of sinners affect the righteous as well as the wicked.

"Away with sinful, earthly things; deaden the evil desires lurking within you; have nothing to do with sexual sin, impurity, lust and shameful desires; don't worship the things of this life; for that is idolatry. For God's terrible anger is upon those who do such things" (Colossians 3:5,6 LB).

Booze

One thing that has helped to promote campus immorality is the unrestrained use of drugs and alcohol. The man who may be shy about making advances toward a girl suddenly becomes aggressive when he has had a few drinks. The girls lose their inhibitions and drown the voices of their consciences with cocktails. A favorite trick of homosexuals is to get young men drunk and seduce them. Marijuana and other drugs will also produce the same results. The Bible says: "Woe unto him that giveth his neighbor drink, puttest thy bottle to him, and maketh him drunken also, that thou mayest look on their nakedness" (Habakkuk 2:15).

On campus drinking beer is almost as common as drinking water. It has become a way of life to both girls and boys as thousands flock to Friday and Saturday night parties to get "wasted." I have arrived on campus at the University of Cincinnati and found students drinking beer outside the union building on Monday morning. Many campuses have bars in the student union.

When we warn against the sin of drunkenness the students immediately try to make Jesus a bartender. As far as they are concerned the only miracle the Lord ever performed was to turn the water into wine. That is their excuse to flood their bodies with poison, make complete fools of themselves and even risk lives so they can "feel good." Few have ever considered WHY Jesus turned the water to wine.

"This beginning of miracles did Jesus in Cana of Galilee, and

manifested forth his glory; and his disciples believed on him"
(John 2:11). Jesus performed this miracle to prove his Deity to
the disciples. If the students really believed Jesus turned water
to wine they would trust in him as the Messiah, the Son of God,
the Savior of the world. They would come to him for the Living
Water and never thirst again. "They would not be drunk on wine
wherein in excess; but be filled with the spirit" (Ephesians
5:18).

Do you mean I'm going to hell for drinking a glass of wine with
a meal or having a cold beer on a hot day?" they always ask.

If I press them they will usually admit they do not stop with
one. That is why the Bible warns, "Wine is a mocker, strong
drink is raging: and whosoever is deceived thereby is not wise"
(Proverbs 20:1). "Look not thou upon the wine when it is red,
when it giveth his colour in the cup, when it moveth itself aright.
At the last it biteth like a serpent and stingeth like an adder"
(Proverbs 23:31,32).

Most students would be far better if they had never seen a
drop of alcohol. What has become a way of life will soon
become a way of death and their good times will produce a
miserable eternity. The same is true for the drug users.

Drugs

Drugs have been a major problem at universities ever since
the late sixties. When I was living in Berkeley during this period,
Timothy Leary, who had been fired from Harvard for his L.S.D.
experiments, was teaching at the free university in the community. He lectured on the effects of L.S.D.

Medical science teaches that one hallucinates under L.S.D.;
that is, they see things that are not there. However, medical
science does not understand the spiritual dimension of an
L.S.D. trip. Leary taught that one sees things that are there; only
they are not in the material, physical world, but the spiritual.
Leary was a sorcerer.

One of the primary tools of a sorcerer is L.S.D. and other

mind-altering drugs. In some inexplicable way L.S.D. enables the user to be transferred (trip) from the natural, physical plane to the supernatural, spiritual plane. As a result of my L.S.D. experiments I became more spiritually minded and actually believed I was getting closer to God. I did not understand that the spiritual world I had contacted was evil. The Bible revealed to me a cosmos made up of God and his host of angels and the devil and his host of demons. When the Spirit of God opened my mind with the tool of his WORD, I renounced the devil and his demons.

Most students may not realize that when they use drugs they are practicing sorcery. Sorcery comes from the Greek word *pharmakeia* which in English would be pharmacy or drugs. Anyone using drugs illicitly is practicing sorcery. Revelation 21:8 warns that all "sorcerers shall have their part in the lake which burneth with brimstone: which is the second death."

Rock 'N Roll

A chapter on lust, booze and drugs would not be complete without the mention of rock 'n roll music. They are all tied together weaving a devilish net for the undiscerning youth. Most college students lost their virginity under the influence of drugs and/or booze while listening to rock 'n roll music.

"Lord, I'll give up my marijuana and alcohol, but I'm not giving up my rock 'n roll." This prayer came from a young man at the University of Florida who was asking God to save him. Sister Cindy had witnessed to this student on the library plaza before his physics class. He admitted he needed to repent but said he had to go to class first. As he walked to class the Holy Spirit told him to go back to the plaza and get right with God or he would die. After ministering to the man for awhile, she joined hands and prayed with him. Suddenly the Holy Spirit uttered that there was something the sinner refused to forsake; and if he did not give it up he would not be converted. The Spirit had spoken the very moment that the student was silently insisting on keeping his Rock 'n Roll. Convinced that God had put the

finger on his sin, the young man forsook his idol and was wonderfully saved and filled with the Spirit. When Sister Cindy
returned a year later the convert was strong in the faith and
working with a local campus church.

This student's intense love for Rock 'n Roll music was not an
isolated case. This abominable music has captured the hearts of
our youth. Most students can quote more lyrics to rock music
than Bible verses. They prefer the devil's encouragement to
selfishness, rather than Jesus' exhortation to self-denial. They
display their idolatry with T-shirts, stickers and posters that say
"Rock Lives," "Rock 'n Roll Shall Never Die" and "Rock is
Forever." Like Baal worshippers of old they attribute deity to an
idol that can never give life.

Some argue that rock music is "just innocent love songs." But
in the sixties they sang "I want to hold your hand," in the
seventies, "Let's spend the night together," and in the eighties,
"I want to kiss you all over." What started out as supposed
innocence has become glorified perversion. Rock idols admit
that when they say love they really mean lust. Face it, when the
Beatles sang "Let's Do It in the Road," they weren't talking
about driving their Rolls Royce down the highway.

Many rock groups are blatantly blasphemous and satanic.
Even some of their names defy God: like Black Sabbath and
Grateful Dead. Mick Jagger sings, "Sympathy for the Devil"
and one of Van Halen's greatest hits is, "Running With the
Devil."

Other singers are more subtle. The lie of the typical pop rock
song is, "meet the right person, have a good sex life and you'll
live happily ever after."

Sonny and Cher sang "All I Ever Need Is You," and "I've
Got You, Babe." Today they are divorced. Obviously they
needed more than each other. They needed a relationship with
the God of the universe.

This generation loves Rock 'n Roll because it has a message
they can relate to: SEX, DRUGS and PARTY.

Years ago when I was a Rock 'n Roll hippie freak, Mick
Jagger came out with the song, "I Can't Get No Satisfaction."

It became a top hit and is still popular over a decade later. Why? Because with all their dope, lust and partying this generation is still not satisfied.

Mick Jagger, for instance, is a multimillionaire, he has fame, fortune, sex and drugs yet the best song he can sing is "I Can't Get No Satisfaction;" because there is no contentment in sin.

The Christian can not relate to music that glorifies sin. They hate sin and therefore they hate rock music. Jagger's song could never appeal to the believer who has peace that passes understanding. We sing with King David, the greatest songwriter who ever lived, "The Lord is my Shepherd I Shall Not Want."

Fraternities and Sororities

The Greek social organizations encourage this decadent lifestyle more than any institution on campus. Having been a member of a fraternity, as an undergraduate, I can speak from experience. In the early 60s women still had hours: 10:30 p.m. on week days and 1:00 a.m. on weekends. The opposite sex was never allowed in student rooms. Therefore, in the basement of the Delta Upsilon house at Indiana University, we had what we called the "dark room." This was not a place for developing film. In the "dark room" there was neither light nor window, the walls were painted black and lined with thickly cushioned leather couches. The floor was carpeted with old, stained mattresses out of the dormitory.

We used to have exchange dinners with the sorority houses. Initially, we would play the role of gentlemen to put them off guard. But soon we were drawing beer from a keg in order to **break down their wills. When we paired off with one we would lead her into the "darkroom" and shut the door. Propriety will** not allow me to detail what happened next. However, I will say many a sorority girl was over exposed in the "darkroom" to the background music of Johnnie Mathis.

A quarter-century later Greek life is more debased than ever. I understand they don't have the darkroom anymore at the Delta

Upsilon house. It is now a mere storage room. Of course it's obsolete today in this era of coed dorms and open visitation. The girls have no hours and frequently spend the night with their boyfriends. Many a student has admitted to me that he joined the fraternity to party. This is not to say all the boys and girls are lawless, just many of them.

Why would any Christian choose to be a part of this life? The Bible warns, "Do not be deceived, bad company corrupts good morals" (I Corinthians 15:33). Professing Christians claim they join the fraternities or sororities to be witnesses. However, in order to live in such a situation eventually they lower their standards instead of raising others to biblical standards. Lot is a classic example.

We are known in the world by the company we keep. Jesus ate and drank with sinners but it was always on his terms. He never lowered his holy and temperate standard in order to be accepted. If the so-called Christians in the fraternities and sororities were really taking the kind of stand they ought to be taking, the organization would either soon be converted or the Christians would be ostracized.

The second commandment forbids idolatry. An idol is anything we put ahead of God.

A boy boldly walked into the middle of a crowd encircling me and said, "You have been making derogatory remarks about my fraternity. I am a Christian and lead a Bible study in my house; I don't appreciate your condemning of us."

"God's name has been blasphemed for several days by this crowd," I replied, "Yet that does not bother you. I say something critical about your fraternity and you quickly come to its defense, you refuse to stand up for truth. Young man your fraternity is an idol in your life. Repent or God will spue you out of his mouth."

If the believers on campus were as dedicated to working for the Kingdom of God as the Greeks are in promoting their organizations there would be revival. We are social beings and we need fellowship. This is one of the main reasons God has established the local church. If Christians were as active in the local church as they ought to be, there would be no time for these social groups.

"Be ye not unequally yoked together with unbelievers; for what fellowship hath righteousness with unrighteousness? And what communion hath light with darkness? Wherefore come out from among them, and be ye separate, saith the Lord, and touch not the unclean thing; and I will receive you" (II Corinthians 6:14,17).

Many who attended the Jimmy Carter rally at the free speech forum were treated to a dose of old-time religion, but it was not coming from the democratic candidate.
— The Daily Egyptian

12

IN THE NEWS

In October of 1976, Max Lynch and I were preaching in Illinois and discussing the presidential election between Jimmy Carter and Gerald Ford.

Brother Max said, "Wouldn't it be great if we could preach to the candidates?"

"Why not," I thought. Moses preached to Pharaoh, Elijah to King Ahab, John the Baptist to Herod, Paul to King Agrippa. Why couldn't we preach to these great men?

The next day we went to Southern Illinois University. When we arrived at the free speech area a crowd of thousands had gathered. Upon inquiry we found out that candidate Jimmy Carter was scheduled to speak at noon. An open-air platform had been built for the occasion. We circled the crowd praying in the spirit and finally stoped under a big oak tree behind the platform.

Brother Max said, "Here, Brother Jed, hold my Bible." Then he began to climb the tree. Soon he was high in the tree, mostly covered from sight by the fall foliage. Soon, the Carter entourage, with some of the top state and local politicians, drove up in limousines. They took the platform and when Jimmy Carter opened his mouth to begin his speech a voice from the tree top cried, "REPENT!"

Carter was startled. I could imagine the secret service reaching for their guns.

Carter addressed what he considered the issues: inflation and unemployment.

But Brother Max yelled, "What about abortion? What about the rising crime rate? What about drunkenness and dope addiction? What about divorce?" Brother Max knew that these and other sins were leading to the breakdown of American society. He wanted the professing "born again" candidate to address the sin issue. Jimmy Carter had nothing about sin in his notes and, becoming very frustrated, he cut his speech short. He and the other politicians then sped away from the scene.

Hundreds of people gathered under the tree to see who had interrupted their political rally. Several were so enraged that they climbed the tree determined to get him down. One woman got out on a limb and grabbed Brother Max's coattails, attempting to pull him from the tree. He became concerned about the woman's safety so agreed to come down if she would stop pulling.

When Brother Max dropped from the lowest limb, the police had to form a wedge to whisk him away from the angry crowd. They took him into a room in the administration building until the crowd dispersed.

Then I began preaching at another location on campus and many regathered to listen.

The next day Brother Max's feat received the main headline in the newspaper, VOICE FROM THE TREE TOP CRIES "REPENT!" A photograph pictured him with a broad smile as the police were escorting him away from the mob. Candidate Carter took a back seat in the news. Thanks to Brother Max's stand and the media coverage, the students' attention turned from politics to the Word of God.

Mission accomplished!

Radicals Versus The U.S. Navy and Special Forces

The treetop incident is just one of the occasions when we have been able to upstage other events which the media had planned to cover. Typically, it was the result of a spontaneous move of the Holy Spirit and no premeditation on our part.

The same was true when we arrived at the University of Oregon in 1984 and found about 25 students protesting around the U.S. Navy recruiting table. The rebels were armed with propaganda signs, gory war pictures and a volunteer who laid in front of the Navy table with ketchup on his body. Most students were ignoring them but as the TV cameras arrived, Cindy started calling the protesters sissies, cowards and socialist dupes. Within seconds a crowd of 100 had gathered.

I declared, "Peace is very precious to the Christian but freedom is even more precious. The price of liberty is costly. The freedoms we enjoy in this nation were baptized in the blood of Americans at Bull Run, Gettysburg, the Argonne Forest, Corregidor and Vietnam. If we are not willing to support the military that helps defend our liberties then our ancestors shed their blood in vain and there's no hope for our posterity."

We got the headlines on the evening news and in the student newspaper the next day.

Our Largest Crowd

Syracuse, New York has given me the most extensive news coverage. Since Syracuse University is a private institution, I had to get a permit to speak. Reluctantly, the administration granted me a permit from 12-2 p.m. outside of Hendricks Chapel. Campus security watched intently as an estimated crowd of 700 to 800 quickly gathered.

At one point a student threw a pie shell filled with shaving cream into my face. The director of security tackled and detained him. I continued preaching until another student appeared from the crowd, grabbed the Bible from my hand and pitched it into the crowd tearing several pages from it.

Even though I made a deliberate attempt to avoid some of the more provocative issues, the crowd was in an uproar. The emergency medical crew from the university ambulance service had arrived on the scene. The crowd had closed in and it appeared that I would be mobbed. The administration ordered the police to move in and stop me for my own safety. Cries of outrage echoed from the crowd as police and university officials escorted me into the chapel. Eagerly, students reached for my pamphlets as the police whisked me away. When the crowd dispersed, officials took me to my car and I drove on to the University of Massachusetts.

Two years later, in the fall of 1984, I called the Syracuse University chaplain again to request a permit to speak on campus. The administration refused to grant me permission to speak outside because they feared that riotous conditions would result. I was offered the use of Hendricks Chapel. The officials granted me permission to speak outside on the steps of the chapel to draw the students attention and then I had to move inside for the remainder of the afternoon. I contacted the student newspaper and it printed front page notices the day before and the day of my arrival.

There was a crowd of 200 waiting to hear me when I came on campus. Within the alloted 10 minutes the crowd increased to several hundred. About 200 followed me into the chapel and I preached and reasoned with them until 5 p.m. I commanded those who wanted to get right with God to walk to the altar. The chapel went silent as two students answered my call. Michele, a freshman, and Ethan, a sophomore, said they had been saved previously but "backslid" away from God at college. The *Syracuse Post Standard* quoted Michele as saying, "When you go to college and have all this freedom, it's the devil's chance to attack you."

The next day we were disappointed to find that we could not start our meeting until 2 p.m. because the chapel was scheduled for another group. Cindy and I talked of going to another campus because students tend to leave campus early on a Friday afternoon.

We had an interview scheduled with a reporter in the chaplain's office at 12:30 p.m. so I decided to keep the appointment and supposed we might have a good teaching session with a small crowd of interested students afterwards in the chapel.

When I opened the chapel door at 1:45 p.m. to step outside, I was stunned to see 2,000 students covering about half the quadrangle and another 200 on the steps waiting to hear me. This was the largest crowd ever in my ministry.

I fired both barrels in my alloted 10 minutes and turned and marched through the doors up to the pulpit with the multitudes right behind me. Some were carrying beer and others were smoking. They quickly filled the 1,200 seats in the auditorium and packed the aisles. Police estimated the crowd at 1,500. The fire marshal came out as a safety precaution. Uniformed and plain clothes police were scattered throughout the building and several lined the platform to prevent students from rushing it. The police chief sat in the choir loft overseeing and directing his forces.

Cindy started preaching and a few boys exposed themselves. Three balconies of students were stomping their feet and waving their arms the way fans do at sporting events. The chaplain asked if I really wanted to go through with it. I assured him that we did. He graciously volunteered to try to calm the throng. He reminded the students that I had a right to be heard. I preached and gradually more and more students stopped heckling and started listening.

After two hours we brought all but a dozen students under control. Finally, I used the tactic of divide and conquer. I announced that Cindy would take questions from the girls at the pulpit left of the platform and I would answer the boy's questions at the right.

When a few of the boys went over to Cindy's side, she answered one of their questions. The girls immediately chastised her for disobeying my instructions in taking a question from a boy.

Cindy retorted, "I can make an exception for him because he is a sissy. That is why he is over here with the girls."

Cindy continued to battle with some contentious women.

I had a crowd of attentive men until our permit expired at 5 p.m. As we wearily walked down the chapel steps several students congratulated us for our stand.

We marched on to the University of Vermont.

One reason a relatively few radical students and professors in the 60s were successful in transforming the campuses was because they were able to get extensive media coverage. Typically, our preaching will be the leading news story in the campus daily and often we receive front-page coverage in the city newspaper.

Below are just a few headlines from the hundreds of articles that have been written about us over the last decade:

★ SMOCK BRINGS FIRE AND BRIMSTONE TO SAVE STUDENTS, *The Daily Collegian*, October 8, 1979.

★ PREACHER JED INSPIRES THE WORST IN HIS CONGREGATION, *Arizona Daily Wildcat*, February 28, 1978.

★ 1000 LISTEN TO GOSPEL, *College Heights Herald*, October 2, 1982.

★ JED SMOCK, "HOLY ROLLERS" STILL ROLLING AT OU, *Athens Post*, May 25, 1984.

★ JED AND CINDY: HUCKSTERS FOR GOD, *Arizona Daily Wildcat*, February 16, 1984.

★ EVANGELISTS FILL A NEED, *Daily Titan*, February 9, 1984.

★JED SMOCK MESSENGER OF GOD? *The Cornell Daily Sun,* October 18, 1979.

★THE PREACHER AND THE DAMNED, *Rutgers Targum,* October 15, 1979.

★PREACHER MAN COMES TO SAVE CSUF FROM HELL, *The Daily Collegian,* March 21, 1980.

★FIERY SERMON RIPS STUDENTS, DAMNS LIFE-STYLE, *The University Daily Kansan,* August 18, 1980.

★VISITING EVANGELIST TKO'S STUDENT HECK-LERS, *The Daily Cougar,* January 22, 1980.

★JED SMOCK HAS RETURNED, *The Kentucky Kernel,* November 10, 1981.

★BROTHER SMOCK CREATES CONTROVERSY, *The Asbury Collegian,* November 11, 1981.

★BROTHER JED CASTIGATES STUDENTS; THEY LOVE IT, *Minneapolis Tribune,* June 6, 1982.

★DYNAMIC DUO DRAWS CROWD OF HECKLING, HISSING "SINNERS," *The Lumberjack,* April 11, 1984.

★EVANGELIST SUFFERS VERBAL, PHYSICAL ABUSE, *The Daily Orange,* October 4, 1982.

★PREACHERS THROWN IN JAIL, *Daily Kent Stater,* September 16, 1982.

Besides the news articles, letters to the editor, pro and con, will follow for days. Once a friend sent me a total of 21 articles and letters written to the editor over a three-week period. They were the result of three days of ministry at Penn State. These articles and letters are like putting a tract in the hand of each student, faculty member and administrator.

At the University of Florida, a heckler tried to steal my billfold out of my back pocket. I turned and kicked him in the pants as he took off running. An alert photographer snapped the picture and it appeared the next day in *The Gainsville Sun* along with an article. The end of the article stated that "Rev. Smock will be speaking at the Holiday Inn at 7:30 p.m. tonight." This was $200 worth of free publicity for my meeting! A number of townspeople came out that night who otherwise would not have known about the service.

It is not unusual for local T.V. news to cover us and national evening news has televised me twice. Frequently I have been interviewed on call-in radio programs. The highlight of media coverage was in May, 1983, in the campus edition of *Newsweek Magazine. Newsweek* acknowledged that both Sister Cindy and I are making a regular circuit on campuses. The magazine published a colored picture of me "raising God's army and battling for souls at the University of Texas, Austin."

Pat Robertson and Jim Bakker have been gracious enough to invite me on the 700 Club and P.T.L. Club. Many local radio and television ministries have interviewed me. My testimony has been published in *Voice Magazine*, The Gideons International magazine, the *Texas Herald Magazine* and *Power Magazine*. The coverage by the Christian media has enabled me to exhort Christians to be bolder in their witness.

Today's headlines, of course, wrap tomorrow's garbage. Therefore, eternity may prove the most effective media coverage to be the college year books. We have received pages of displays in numerous annuals. People do not throw away their yearbooks. One can imagine a student 20 years after graduation thumbing through his annual and seeing a picture of Brother Jed preaching and the Holy Spirit using this to quicken the Word to his mind and convict his heart.

The Smock family going to Sunday church service in 1952. From left, James, George Jr., George E., William, Charlotte and Catherine.

Jed leaves Terre Haute, Indiana, for Morocco, North Africa, in November of 1971. This was during his hippie days.

Yearbook photo by Gary Harwood

KSU Police sergeant Bill Shanafelt and patrolman Missy Wilson lead traveling evangelist James Gilles from the Student Center.

Traveling preachers locked up

By DONN HANDY
Stater Staff Writer

The "Gospel according to Jed" was delivered to KSU students again yesterday, and this time audience reaction was so inflamed that the wandering evangelist is now in jail as the result.

The Rev. George "Jed" Smock, 39, of Terre Haute, Ind., and his companion, James G. Gilles, 20, of Evansville, Ind., were arrested late yesterday afternoon on charges of disorderly conduct by KSU police after several hours of preaching to hundreds of assembled students which led to near violent actions.

Smock and Gilles were held overnight in the Portage County Jail, each on $2,500 bonds, and were to

have a hearing today.

Police also cited a KSU student, Alan N. Silverman of 210 N. Sherman St., Kent, for disorderly conduct after he allegedly began shoving Smock for the evangelist's remarks about Jews. Police are also looking for a woman who apparently slapped Smock.

FOR THE second day in a row, the evangelists moved into the Student Center Plaza shortly after noon, began preaching, and quickly drew a crowd of a few serious listeners and a lot of hecklers. Apparently, the evangelists exacerbated the crowd much more blatantly yesterday, focusing their attacks on youth morality.

(See 'Preachers,' Page 2)

The Kent State University crowd became so angry at Jed's preaching that campus police arrested both Jed and Jim Gilles, who was traveling with Jed on the preaching mission. Above, campus police lead Gilles away from the Student Center.

Jed drew one of the largest crowds of his campus ministry at Syracuse University in Syracuse, New York.

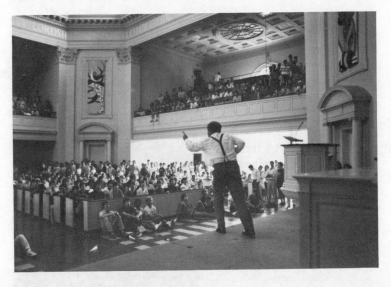

Here he preaches to Syracuse students in the university chapel.

Jed with Pastor Clyde
Swalls shortly after
Jed's conversion in
August of 1971.

"Holy Hubert," though
blind, still preaches on
the college campuses.
Here he is at West
Washington State
University in March
of 1984.

Sister Cindy confronts a hostile crowd at the University of Oklahoma.

These are scenes from Jed's confrontations with angry, hostile and sometimes violent students.

These are scenes from Jed's confrontations with angry, hostile and sometimes violent students.

This cartoon, typical of campus newspaper coverage of The Campus Ministry, pans Jed's preaching on the campus.

The wierd appearance of these students is typical of some of the strange looks and behavior of the students Jed confronts on almost a daily basis.

Going after sinners

Evangelists heckled at OSU

By Pat Kight
of the Gazette-Times

"Turn from all your sins right now! Turn to Jesus Christ!" screamed Cindy Smock, clutching a leatherette-covered Bible in one hand and raising the other heavenward.

Obscenities showered down on her, chanted by the mostly male crowd encircling her.

Just another Friday afternoon on the Oregon State University quad?

Smock and her husband, traveling evangelist Jed Smock, were the latest in a parade of local and out-of-town crusaders who've brought their impromptu revival meetings to the grassy lawn in front of OSU's Memorial Union.

So commonplace have such preachers become that they are ignored by the thousands of OSU students who cross the quad on their way to and from classes.

But the Smocks were hard to ignore — as were the hordes of jeering students who surrounded them.

With a fiery and a "repent-or-be-damned" preaching style, the couple took turns all afternoon exhorting the students to abandon "sex, drugs and perversion" and seek salvation through Jesus Christ.

In response, they got hoots of derision, irate challenges and shouted obscenities.

Jed preaches at Oregon State University in Corvallis in April of 1984. Both he and Sister Cindy were heckled and had obscenities shouted at them.

Prior to her marriage to Jed in July of 1983, Sister Cindy bravely traveled on her own to preach on university campuses.

Here Sister Cindy pauses to take questions from the university students. Her countenance reveals the soberness of her mission.

Max Lynch has preached so regularly at Purdue University that some consider him the campus chaplain.

Jed's church ministry produced campus evangelist Jim Gilles — a powerfully anointed minister to students.

Sister Pat confronts angry Moslem students at the University of Arkansas. She finally subdued them and they became attentive to her preaching of God's Word.

Brother Jed points out sin at California State University in Chico but the students strongly resist the truth.

Grace and law confront one another at Oregon State University.

Jed stands firm on the Word of God as he confronts a student.

Brother Jed preaches indoors (above) and outdoors (below) to Purdue University students in West Lafayette, Indiana.

This punk rocker said "I love you dead, Jed."

Some students laugh and joke, even when the Gospel is being preached.

*Beside those things that are
without . . . the care of the churches
— II Corinthians 12:28.*

13

SIN IN THE CAMP

In the heat of the summer, 11 months after my conversion, I rode my 10-speed bicycle 40 miles to preach my first revival meeting in Worthington, Indiana. As the July sun beat down on my brow, I pondered the fact that most of the town's 2,000 residents were peddling to a much hotter eternity. My burden was that several meetings in the storefront Assembly of God Church would pull many out of the fire. Preparing a week of sermons was quite a challenge since, except for my testimony, I did not have a collection of anecdotes to fill in my messages. However, I had been diligently studying the Bible for over a year and had memorized many verses.

Each afternoon I took an hour out of my prayer and Bible study time to ride around town witnessing and inviting people to church. None accepted my invitation. When we closed the meeting at the end of the scheduled week, only one soul had come forward to the altar for salvation. I returned home feeling very troubled about having left Worthington. Four days after we closed the services some church members telephoned to say that they did not think my work was finished. I called the pastor and he suggested that I return and reopen the revival the next Sunday.

The second week my daily witnessing began to produce fruit. Tuesday a group of youth gathered on the sidewalk in front of the church to listen. We had to keep the door open since there was no air conditioning and this offered the only ventilation. Wednesday night there was almost as large a crowd listening from the sidewalk as was sitting in the building. At the end of my message I walked to the door and commanded the youth, "Come in here and give your hearts to God."

To my surprise, eight of them walked in barefooted, some shirtless and fell to their knees. I led each one in a sinner's prayer.

This experience confirmed to me the necessity of the successful evangelist working outside of a building if a community is truly going to be moved. As I have made this my pattern, God has opened the door for me to witness to the small and to the great.

Tennessee Colonel

Impressed with my ministry in Nashville, Tennessee, Governor Winfield Dunn appointed me "Tennessee Colonel and Aid de Camp, Governor's Staff."

This was a testimony to God's amazing grace that a former revolutionary was now being commended for "Patriotism, Valor and Fidelity." Indeed it was evident "old things had passed away" as one who had wanted to overthrow our Republic joined with this god-fearing governor to pray for his administration and the people of the state.

This honor was the result of a two-week revival and outreach held with Rev. W.C. Langford's Belmont Assembly of God Church in the summer of 1974. I preached to the lost at Vanderbilt University, Scarit College and in the "Red Light" district. The mayor's special assistant was baptized in the Holy Spirit and the mayor bestowed upon me the keys of the city.

Across the nation I have emphasized that Christians should be bolder in their witness, that God wanted to make each layman an activist for the cause of Christ. In church after church I preached from my theme text, "WHO WILL RISE UP FOR ME AGAINST THE EVILDOERS OR WHO WILL STAND UP FOR ME AGAINST THE WORKERS OF INIQUITY?" (Psalms 94:16).

Thousands publicly committed themselves to answering this call but only a fragment have followed through. When persecution comes for the Word's sake they burn out. Still, it has been my joy to kindle a perpetual flame for souls in the hearts of a few.

One of these firebrands, Mike Denigan, a prosperous florist and church deacon, has become a constant soulwinner and a blazing open-air preacher on Fountain Square in Cincinnati, Ohio.

Disco Invasion

Mike Denigan was attending my revival meeting in Florence, Kentucky, when God instructed him to go witness in the bars in which he had once caroused. Since so much of my life had been wasted on a bar stool, I was anxious to reach the drunkards. After being banned from the American Legion bar, we invaded the Ramada Inn disco lounge. The blank-faced crowd of career singles and lonely salesmen puffed their cigarettes and sipped their cocktails as the band played an empty "love song." When the band took a break, Mike and his wife, with Cindy and I, walked to the dance floor and, to the surprise of all, started singing to the tune of "Shortnin' Bread:"

> *All God's children love living, living.*
> *All God's children love living bread.*
> *Throw up your hands.*
> *Fall upon your face.*
> *The Holy Ghost is going to shake this place.*

As we sang we acted out the lyrics by throwing up our hands, bowing our faces to the floor and turning around. The Holy Spirit began to shake up the incredulous customers in the disco.

Suddenly the Spirit of God moved within Cindy and she preached: "Awake, ye drunkards and weep and howl for the new wine which is Jesus Christ has been cut off from you. Be not deceived, no drunkard shall inherit the kingdom of God. For all ye drunkards shall burn forever in the LAKE OF Fi-rrrre, except ye REPENT and believe in Jesus."

The crowd was stunned. The Lord had revealed to me that this was to be a hit-and-run operation. We had hit so I grabbed Cindy by the arm and said, "Let's GO." As we dashed out the door a salesman in a three-piece suit leaned over to his associate and said, "I have been all over the world, but now I have truly seen everything."

Our activities were noised abroad and as a result Mike was publicly repudiated from the pulpit of his own church. Regrettably, our churches are filled with fire extinguishers and wet blankets.

A Turning Point

In the Fall of 1978 God showed me why so many professing Christians refuse to be bold witnesses and vehemently oppose those who do take a stand.

The trend during the 1970s in the pentecostal, charismatic and full gospel churches was for ministers to emphasize the new birth, the baptism of the Holy Spirit, faith, both physical and inner healing, deliverance, financial prosperity and prophecy. In the early years of my ministry this was my general course except for the inner healing. My testimony, coupled with campus evangelism, made my ministry unique and therefore in demand by churches and Full Gospel Businessmen's Fellowships. I had always assumed "Christians" were living moral and upright lives because this is what the Bible calls "our reasonable service." But God would soon show me stark reality, the inside of the cup and the platter. He would soon pry open the whited sepulchres and uncover the dead men's bones rankled with maggots and putrefaction.

It happened in what I thought would be a typical engagement in a charismatic church in Georgia. I brought forth a message on holiness and at the end of the sermon, as was my custom, I started to lead 300 people in a positive confession that they were the "righteousness of God in Christ Jesus." But the Holy Spirit checked me and impressed on my mind, "THERE IS SIN IN THE CAMP. THERE IS SIN IN THE CAMP."

Startled, I repeated to the congregation what I had heard from God. "THERE IS SIN IN THE CAMP." Soon the altars was filled with people on their faces before the Lord.

A woman rose from her knees and asked for the pulpit. She publicly confessed to specific personal sins. When she finished, someone else also admitted to particular sins. Then another. The stench and stink of religious hypocrisy began to seep out. Soon people were lined up to come to the platform to confess their transgressions. The tombs were opened wide and all kinds of wickedness and iniquity was exposed by the Holy Spirit. Almost everyone became involved, from the church leadership down to the little children. I was stunned! This was thought to be a spiritual church. All the gifts were supposed to be in operation. It had a Christian Academy, Bible Training Center and a radio and television outreach. The confessions went on and on until almost midnight. God put sinews, flesh and skin upon their bones and breathed within them that they might live and know that he is God. After the Spirit had done his work, I dismissed the congregation.

That night in my room, during a time of prayer, the Holy Spirit revealed to me that this church was typical of congregations where I had been speaking for several years. The same sins that I was crying out against on campus were hiding under the cover of the church pews. Instead of calling the people to repentance, I had been confirming them in their self-righteousness, blindly encouraging each to confess positively that they were "the righteousness of God in Christ Jesus," when in reality they were in rebellion.

That night was to prove a turning point in my ministry.

Repentance

I had to start preaching against sin in the churches. Jesus preached repentance from the throne room to five of the seven churches in Revelation. To the church of the Laodiceans he declared, "as many as I love, I rebuke and chasten: be zealous therefore, and repent."

Most scholars consider the Laodicean assembly to be a type of the last-days church. I had been saying to the modern day Laodiceans that they were "rich, increased with goods and in need of nothing." But the Holy Spirit wanted to expose them "As wretched, and miserable, and poor, and blind, and naked." God intended to use me to purify the churches before the second coming of the Lord as he used John the Baptist to purge Israel before Christ's first advent.

John proclaimed, "The axe is laid unto the root of the trees" (Matthew 3:11). The axe is God's Word, the trees are the people and the root is their sin.

It is common in the charismatic churches to blame everything on the devil. Ministers have gained great popularity by going from meeting to meeting and casting devils out of people who are still bound with sin.

For example, the sin of self-abuse is not "a spirit of lust." It is a refusal to turn from the selfish habit. Likewise, the heart of the liar's problem is his refusal to tell the truth, not a "lying spirit."

People must take responsibility for their behavior. Too many ministers fear offending the sinners. They give professing believers an excuse to sin by saying that demons are the cause. The devil cannot make a Christian sin. He chooses to sin. For deliverance he MUST choose to repent!

Repentance is more than a mere admission of wrongdoing and a sorrow for it. The fornicator may be genuinely sorry for his fornication, especially if he catches the dreaded Herpes II. Repentance implies an understanding of the justice of the commandments of God and of the folly and madness of sin. The repentant sinner recognizes that he is wholly wrong and wicked and that God is wholly right and just. The wicked must see that he deserves nothing but eternal torment in the LAKE of FIRE. He must submit his will to God's will and throw himself on the mercy and grace of God to set him free from the power and dominion of sin. The repentant completely forsakes all sin to walk the highway of holiness. He has a godly sorrow for what his sin has done to God. ALAS, it was sin that nailed the hands of God's beloved Son Jesus Christ to the cross.

After my experience in Georgia, I began to regularly bring forth this message of repentance.

In February of 1979 this preaching revolutionized Praise Chapel in Southern California. As I commanded the congregation to turn from sin and "bring forth fruits meet for repentance," they responded by public confession of their wickedness. As the meetings continued, many brought forth books, rock 'n roll records, immodest clothes and other idols to be destroyed. It reminded me of Paul's great awakening at Ephesus: "Many that believed came, and confessed, and showed their deeds. Many of them also which used curious art brought their books together and burned them before all men." "SO MIGHTILY GREW THE WORD OF GOD AND PREVAILED" (Acts 19:17-19).

True repentance brought true revival to Praise Chapel. The pastor has often said it was a turning point in his fellowship. Many who repented in those meetings have started other strong soulwinning churches in area cities. Today they are the most committed body of believers in Southern California.

I have found this message is generally well-received by church-goers. Many have come up to me after a service and said "This is what we really need to hear." However, there are always a few rebels in the crowd and occasionally the pastor is included.

This was the case when I preached in an Arizona church and the congregation started confessing sin. Saying he objected to public admission of sin, the pastor closed the meeting the next day. Although I had been going to the church for several years, I was no longer welcome.

If there is to be revival, "judgment must begin at the house of God." With revival comes purging. Many ministers and laymen who speak of revival must first allow the convicting ministry of the Holy Spirit to accompany it. I suffered in the spirit for weeks over this rejection but set my face like a flint to proclaim the message God had given me.

A Brand Plucked Out of the Fire

In July 1982 I started a week-long meeting in a "full gospel" church in Evansville, Indiana. My ministry was well known in the city for I had twice addressed the Full Gospel Business Men's Fellowship and had spoken once for the Gideons. I had also been in several of the area churches and ministered in this particular one on a previous occasion.

After three days of strong preaching on repentance, I brought forth a message on the Fear of God. Nightly the congregation had come to the altars to pray. The Holy Spirit was developing a sin consciousness in the church. Suddenly a leading woman in the congregation began to "prophesy."

"All I see is people that love God. That are pure and holy in my eyes . . ." she prophesied.

She went on in this strain for a few minutes. When she stopped all was quiet. This was a crucial point in the meeting. If the church believed this false prophesy, I might as well pack my bags and leave town.

As I prayed for direction, the pastor rose to his feet and walked to the pulpit.

"Brother Smock is right," he said. "There is sin in the camp. We need to repent."

He confessed to sin in his own life. A spirit of contrition seemed to come over the congregation. Others followed the pastor's example.

The next night I took my text from Numbers 25: The young men of Israel committed whoredom with some pagan women who influenced the men to worship idols. An angry God smote the people with a plague and ordered Moses to have the whore-

mongers and idolaters executed. Meanwhile, Zimri, a man of
Israel insolently brought a whore named Cozbi into the camp
before the eyes of Moses and all the people, as they were
repenting at the door of the Tabernacle. When Phinehas, a
young God-fearing Israeli, saw this, he rose up from prayer and
took his javelin to the tent where Zimri was with Cozbi. He
thrust the javelin all the way through the man's body and into the
whore's belly. So the plague was stopped but only after 24,000
people had died.

To dramatize the action for the church, I took an imaginary
javelin in hand, made a flying leap off the platform into the
middle of the congregation and demonstrated Phinehas' execution of judgment. Many were shocked at my performance but I
had effectively illustrated the truth. Little did I know there was a
Zimri in the congregation that night with his Cozbi. During the
worship service he had been lifting his hands high in praise.
James Gilles was his name.

Jim Gilles had been an 18-year-old dope fiend and rock and
roll freak. In November 1980 he had attended a Van Halen rock
concert. In the middle of the performance, group leader David
Lee Roth shouted to the crowd, "Not even God can save your
soul at a Van Halen concert." The crowd of 13,000 people
roared to their feet giving him a standing ovation while yelling
for more blasphemy.

Jim Gilles was stunned at the remark and reaction. As he
contemplated what had happened, the group sang their biggest
hit, "Running With The Devil." Then Jim understood that he
and the whole crowd were gleefully following and worshipping
Satan.

Jim faced the reality that he was headed for hell. He cried out,
"god save my soul right here in the middle of this Van Halen
concert!" Jesus answered his prayer and instantly set him free
from drugs, lust, booze and rock 'n roll. The following Sunday
he went to church and made a public confession of his repentance and faith. The elders laid hands on him and he was
baptized in the Holy Spirit.

Jim warned his girlfriend that they were going to have to stop EVERYTHING.

She responded saying, "Oh Jim! I'm so proud of you."

Little did she know, he had had more than a momentary emotional experience. He had been genuinely converted but the devil was determined to get him back through the girl he was dating.

After he had been attending church for several weeks, the little strumpet whined, "Jim how come you don't love my anymore? You don't touch me like you used to."

Alas, he fell for the oldest line in the book. The irony of the situation is that Jim had used basically the same line to rob the girl of her virtue in the first place. Jim continued to go to church with the girl and make a show of religion. Everyone considered Jim to be one of the outstanding young persons in the congregation.

Jim was shaken that night by the story of Phinehas. He saw how much God hated sin and that he stood condemned before his Creator. At the end of my message Jim ran to the altar to ask God's forgiveness. His girl followed close behind in her designer jeans. Jim's repentance was godly that night but his girl's was merely a worldly sorrow. Regrettably, the javilin of the Word did not reach into her belly.

At the close of my meetings in Evansville, Jim arranged to preach on campus with me during his week of vacation that fall. Jim did a commendable job so I agreed to let him join me for another week the following spring. I was very impressed that a young man would devote his vacation to the work of the Lord.

In the fall of 1982 Jim was sure that God wanted him to rise up against the evildoers on the university campuses of America. He traveled with me that semester and within weeks developed into a strong preacher of righteousness. He quickly learned how to keep the students' attention and God gave him wisdom to confound the gainsayers who had more formal education than he.

After three months of training I felt Jim was ready to travel the campuses on his own. In one year he faithfully proclaimed God's Word on over 100 universities. He suffered great persecution from the authorities and was arrested at least a dozen times. This was quite a test for the young evangelist but he persevered and saw God use the arrests and court cases for his glory.

With no offering plates on campuses, finances can be a problem for a beginning preacher. Nevertheless, Jim showed great initiative in getting church doors opened to his ministry. His work has impressed many dedicated pastors; not only has he received their support, but his preaching and teaching have been a great blessing to the congregations. By age 21 Jim was a man of prayer, a Bible scholar and a theologian who was successfully promoting the Kingdom of God. Let no man despise his youth for he is a great example among the believers!

Revival

Another outstanding event of my church ministry was a one-day meeting which turned into three weeks of soul-searching services in the largest New Jersey Assembly of God Church. Pastored by Paul Graben, the small Burlington Assembly had experienced rapid growth in the early 70s when several hippies were converted and started bringing in their friends and relatives. At that time the church had a burning zeal for evangelism but during the last few years many had married, had children, started careers and gotten bogged down in the everyday cares of this world.

On a Sunday in October of 1982 I rekindled this lukewarm congregation with what has become my classic text, "WHO WILL RISE UP FOR ME AGAINST THE EVILDOERS OR WHO WILL STAND UP FOR ME AGAINST THE WORKERS OF INIQUITY?" (Psalms 94:16). Many recognized they had lost their first love and they made a new commitment to bring Christ to the world.

The pastor was so impressed with my message and the move of the Holy Spirit that he invited me to return Monday night for a special service. Two hundred people hungry for truth came to this impromptu meeting. I began to hammer against sin, the Holy Spirit fell and there was great conviction in our midst. Many got right with God as I nightly expounded on themes like True and False Repentance, Fear of God, Love of God, Christian Perfection, Holiness, Sanctification, God's Judgment and Suffering for Christ's Sake. Many remarked, "We've never heard it on this wise," and Pastor Graben called the messages "masterpieces."

Even so, not everyone wanted the truth that would set them free. Almost nightly the pastor would inform me of the opposition he was getting from certain church elements. They wanted to find out how long I would be there so they would know when it was "safe" to go back to church. However, he stood steadfast in support and some of the initial rebels came to repentance. A large nucleus received the greatest blessing one may obtain from their Creator: "God sent His Son Jesus to bless you, in turning away everyone of you from his iniquities" (Acts 4:26). This is the last blessing that most blessing seekers desire or even want to hear.

The revival poured into the church's Christian Academy as I preached in their morning chapel services. Students and teachers consecrated their lives to God and had a new fervor for soulwinning. They became eager volunteers to join in my afternoon warfare on the area college campuses. Often up to 40 students, teachers and church members allied with me; and even the younger ones gave a bold witness to the faith of Jesus Christ. Seeing the gross iniquity and utter blindness of the university community, these Christians' eyes were opened to the dire need to raise up a standard of righteousness in our nation.

Tent Meeting

Tapes of this revival were circulated around the country, even reaching the small town of Riverdale, California. Rev. Charles Spencer had become concerned because his denomination had abandoned the old paths of righteousness and holiness and rejected the standard of God's moral law.

The virus of worldly compromise had poisoned churches all over the state until Brother Spencer was the lone pastor in his organization who had not been contaminated. Hearing the tapes from my meeting in New Jersey, he determined to bring me to Riverdale to be the morning speaker in a Bible Holiness Tent Campmeeting.

He mailed prescriptive circulars to FULLY afflicted GOSPEL churches all over California, hoping sick shepherds would respond. But, the phthisical pastors quarantined themselves in their consumptive churches, refusing the Balm of Holiness.

Each morning I inoculated ailing believers from all over the San Joaquin Valley with the Holy Word. I gave them God's vaccine against unhealthy living: simply obey the light you have from a right intention of heart.

The evening speaker was Rev. Bill Burkett, a noted campmeeting teacher and the founder of World Commission, an international missionary outreach. We were amazed to discover that God had revealed to both of us the same antidote to heal sin-diseased Christendom. The titles, themes and applications of our sermons were wonderously alike.

Throughout the years I have found few ministers who would accompany me to a campus. Their excuse is, "That is not my calling, brother." However both Brother Burkett and Brother Spenser preached with me at Fresno State University near Riverdale.

Mountain Moving in the Ozarks

Brother Burkett eagerly promoted my ministry amongst independent pentecostal holiness pastors and denominational ministers who are resisting the abscess of antinomianism. One of his friends, Rev. D.C. Branham, an Assembly of God pastor and Founder-President of Ozark Bible Institute in Neosho, Missouri, invited me to be the afternoon speaker in his annual Holiness Convocation. I preached one of the greatest sermons God has given me to this 1,000 people: "Walking in the Spirit."

This message is the result of extensive prayer and study of Romans 7 and 8. Many agree these are two of the most challenging and perplexing chapters in the Bible. Rev. Burkett says, "They are perplexed because they don't like the challenge."

As I expounded, the Spirit proved that Romans 7 could not possibly refer to a Christian experience. The altars became filled with students, laymen and pastors who chose to walk out of the legalistic defeat of struggling to obey God with a carnal mind; into Romans 8, the spiritual victory of freedom from sin by submitting the renewed mind and will to obey God.

Christians attending the convocation and students from Ozark Bible Institute accompanied us to Missouri Southern State College in nearby Joplin to preach. Friday afternoon classes had been dismissed so students could attend a pep rally and queen coronation which were part of the scheduled homecoming activities.

Sister Cindy's preaching immediately captured a crowd of 250 who quickly forgot about the pep rally. The frustrated miniskirted cheerleaders came outside and attempted, to no avail, to divert the attention of the students from the Gospel message. Finally, to stifle the preaching, the police stopped Cindy and threatened arrest. I quickly took over. The administration recognized the futility of removing over 50 fired-up Christians and reluctantly allowed us to continue.

On Saturday the *Joplin Globe*, which had been on campus to cover homecoming activities, instead gave coverage to our ministry with a front page headline, article and picture: "Preachers Rail at Students at Southern." When we returned Monday, a local T.V. news team had their cameras set up to telecast the event. Our ministry provoked several pro and con letters to the editor.

Many of the so-called Christian students and several of the local pastors were infuriated by our bold approach. None denied our message was true but they condemned our straightforward method of labeling sin and commanding the wicked to repent. A local pastor wrote a letter to the college and city newspapers disassociating himself from our ministry and apologizing to the community for our actions:

> We want you to know that we strongly support
> MSSC (the college) and appreciate the faculty and
> student body. Both my wife and myself are former stu-
> dents there, our daughter is a student now, and our son
> and associate pastor is soon to be graduated. A goodly
> number of young people from our congregation are
> current students.

This is typical of the compromising spirit we find among
many pastors. How can a man of God "strongly support" a
secular college that teaches the lies of evolution, humanism and
socialism? He was so concerned about us offending the wicked.
What about the way the sinner daily offends God?

As we preached the Gospel on that campus many mocked
and laughed at the Word of God. Why was this pastor not
concerned about the name of Jesus which was blasphemed,
ridiculed and scorned by hundreds of students? Part of the
answer is that he was schooled and brainwashed for four years
by a godless college. He would profit by enrolling himself and
family in Ozark Bible Institute.

Another pastor wrote to the city editor commending our
ministry:

> About the preachers at Missouri Southern State
> College:
> I say it is about time. We ministers tend to sit back
> and be comfortable and play the game of not offending
> anybody. If the first church began like that, then no one
> today would know the salvation of Jesus Christ.
> Naturally, the response to being rightfully confronted
> as sinners was not going to be accepted by many. How
> would you feel if someone brought to your attention
> your failures? But this message has to get out. Sexual
> immorality and other sins have become normal on col-
> lege campuses and in society in general.

The sinner who said that he didn't believe in pushing religion on other people apparently had the freedom like the others to walk away from the preaching.

In response to the statement from the Baptist to the effect that the preachers were not doing it the right way, I would like to ask him if his way of not doing it at all was better.

In spite of much questioning and criticizing from local pastors, Brother Branham stood with us. Since this criticism incident we have worked with many independent Pentecostal Holiness churches and found the pastors and congregations some of the most eager to witness and preach with us on campuses.

14

COURTSHIP
AND MARRIAGE

The night before Cindy's conversion the Lord had awakened
me from a sound sleep to pray for her. As I prayed I believed the
Lord was going to save her and had a great work for her to do. I
didn't know what his work would be but I considered the
possibility that he might be preparing her to be my wife.
However, God's plan was to be even bigger than this. Within a
year after her conversion and call to preach, Cindy had become
one of the outstanding women preachers in the nation. "Holy
Hubert" called her a female Billy Sunday.

Cindy and I began to spend much time together in prayer,
Bible study, fellowship and ministry. I had observed a tendency
in some women preachers to be masculine in manner and
attitude. Therefore, I constantly consulted and prayed with
Cindy about the necessity of developing "a meek and quiet
spirit," but one that would be bold in the proclamation of the
Gospel. The Lord did such a marvelous work of grace that
people who have met her and never heard her preach are

incredulous when she lifts up her voice to sound the trumpet of repentance.

Newspaper reporters constantly affirm that it is a different Cindy they interview than the one crying out against sin in the center of campus!

Mark J. Green in *The Daily Collegian* at Penn State wrote: "I took Cindy aside for an interview. She was not the wild and strong damning machine I had seen outside on the steps of Schwab Auditorium. She was a shy, young girl from Florida. Her voice was soft and kind. The only similarity between the two Cindys was the eyes. They were fiery and kind. I told a friend that day that I supposed Christ had eyes like hers."

Why I Married Cindy

Generally God wants people to marry and raise a family but the scriptures also teach the advantages of the single life because the married person may be distracted from the Lord's service by family responsibilities. Cindy and I had deep feeling and regard for one another and soon began to consider the possibility of marriage. We sought the Lord's guidance and wanted only to marry if it would further the cause of the kingdom.

We were very content in our single lives and completely occupied with our ministry.

Solomon wrote, "that favor is deceitful and beauty is vain, but a woman that feareth the Lord she shall be praised" (Proverbs 31:30). Although King Solomon traveled widely and searched diligently in looking for the wise and upright, he concluded: "One man among a thousand have I found; but a woman among all those have I not found" (Ecclesiastes 7:28). This is tragic considering Solomon had over a thousand wives and concubines.

Over the years I had met thousands of pretty single girls on campus and in the churches but Cindy was by far the most God-fearing woman that I had met. Not only was she attractive but she wished to do nothing that would displease God. I knew Cindy fulfilled Solomon's quest; she was one in a thousand!

Since Cindy and I had the same call and vision for the ministry, possible family distractions seemed likely to be minimal and were outweighed by the benefit of a life long holy alliance to advance the cause of Christ. It only remained for God to join together in the flesh what he had already brought together in the Spirit. I had not seen Cindy for about three months because we were in different parts of the country. But we did talk regularly over the telephone, although marriage was not mentioned. We had planned to meet at my mother's in June. A few weeks before I had decided it was time to ask Cindy if she would marry me.

The traditional picture of a marriage proposal has the man on one knee with the woman sitting before him. I thought for this all-important occasion we should both be on our knees before the Lord. I started praying for several minutes.

Finally, I said, "Cindy, I believe it is time to ask the Lord to join us together in the state of holy matrimony."

She looked at me startled and we both returned to prayer.

After a few minutes I asked, "What do you think?"

"Yes," she answered.

I had always boasted on campus that my mother was the number one woman in all of Christendom. When we made the announcement of our engagment to mother, I had to inform her that she had just fallen to number two. Cindy is now number one.

"That is the way it should be," mother replied.

The Right Contract

Rev. Clyde Swalls from Port Charlotte, Florida, performed the ceremony six weeks later at Centenary United Methodist Church in Terre Haute, Indiana, on July 30, 1983. Many ministers today wrongly have the bride and groom repeating the same vows. Cindy and I affirmed the traditional vows which agree with scriptural teachings. I pledged to love, honor and cherish Cindy. She promises to love, honor and obey me.

My lawyer friend, Tom Elkins, always says, "It is crucial that the contract be made upright."

The Bible says, "Wives, submit yourselves unto your own husbands, as it is fit in the Lord. Husbands, love your wives, and be not bitter against them." (Colossians 3:18, 19). The wife expresses her love to her husband by being subject to him. Any woman who does not obey her husband does not love her husband. Nor does she love God because if she loved God, she would keep his commandments. The rebellious wife may have emotional feelings for God and her husband; but where there is not obedience, there is not true love.

Since we have been married, Cindy has not disobeyed me once! By God's grace I have not failed to cherish her and give honor to her as the weaker vessel. We are heirs together of the gracious gift of life. I love her as Christ loved the church and gave himself for it.

A Real Man

When I mention the words submit or obey your husband to this generation of contentious women they howl and rage. In order to pacify them I declare, "I can't blame you girls for not wanting to submit to one of these drunken fraternity boys, or drug crazed hippies, or sex fiends, or rock 'n roll freaks. But girls, when you find a real man, you will have a different attitude about this doctrine of submission. For an example, someone like Sister Cindy found!"

The crowd laughs, several scream, "Just what is a real man?"

"A real man is temperate. He has self control. He is able to restrain his natural appetites and desires. Real men don't drink, use dope or swear. They enter the marriage relationship as virgins. Real men don't listen to Michael Jackson, Boy George or other rock freaks. A real man is one who is able to love and be loved, to satisfy and be satisfied with one woman throughout his life. Most boys on this campus don't qualify as real men because you don't become a real man or real woman until you become a Christian."

How to Find the Right One

My advice to anyone considering a marriage partner is to observe how the individual regards his parents. Does he honor and obey his father? Is he kindly and tender towards his mother?

Girl, the way the boy treats his mother will be the manner in which he will treat you. Boy, does the girl you are interested in honor and obey her father? If she does not, you can be sure that she will never honor or obey you. Does she lie to her parents? If she does, she will cheat on you.

Usually when men are considering a potential wife they first give attention to whether she has a pretty face and a good figure. Next they give consideration to her personality. Usually women first consider the men's personality; second, his liklihood of success; and third, his looks. But boys, that fair face will develop wrinkles and that sharp chin will become double. Her youthful appearance will fade and her slimness is likely to turn to fat.

Girls, if he continues that heavy drinking or drug use those dreams of happiness and success will turn to nightmares. Nine out of 10 wife beaters are drunkards and or dope fiends. As for the nice personality, I have known murderers and thiefs that have nice personalities. There is no virtue in a personality.

There is virtue in character. Character is of primary importance when choosing a mate. Is the individual a person of sound ethics and good moral principles? Alas! Virtue, character ethics, morals and principles are words rarely heard anymore around a college campus. Physical beauty fades with the passing of years; but an excellent character improves and brightens the countenance as the years go by.

A troubled girl asked Cindy, "How do I know if I should marry this man?"

Cindy replied, "Ask him one question? Do you sin? If he sins, don't marry him."

People of good character obey God's Moral Law. Individuals of bad character disobey God's Law.

According to my surveys, most students still consider adultery to be wrong. Any individual considering fidelity in marriage desirable should be sure to marry a virgin. If the man you marry was promisicuous before marriage, matrimony will not suddenly change him. If he never learned to control his appetites before marriage, when faced with temptation after marriage, sooner or later he will succumb. On the other hand, if he has controlled his desires before marriage he is likely to control them when faced with temptation after the union.

The most important element in a successful marriage is trust. If he even tried to have intimate relations with you before marriage, you have no basis upon which to believe he will not try to have illegitimate relations afterwards. The next girl may not play so hard to get. This lack of trust may result in a bitter jealousy. This jealousy will eventually destroy the marriage. These principles apply to the woman as well.

The purpose of courtship is to establish a relationship in the spiritual, mental and social realms. However, most young people today quickly get involved physically and that becomes the basis of the relationship. Thinking they are compatible, some go on to marriage. You can be physically harmonious with any healthy person of the opposite sex; but it takes more than physical attraction to hold a marriage together. The couple soon discovers that they do not have physical relations every night. Suddenly they realize that they need to communicate with each other but they have married strangers with different values, morals and interests. As a result the couple eventually gives up and gets a divorce.

It is not advisable to even court someone with whom you have fundamental spiritual differences. Especially if the person is of a different religion. It is best to find someone in the same church or denomination. **For example, a Protestant and Catholic should** not court. If you discover someone with the same religious beliefs and you start a relationship, develop it on the spiritual plane by praying, reading the Bible, ministering, visiting orphans and widows and going to church. Stay away from picture shows, bars, dances, rock concerts, etc. Actually, if the boy even suggests a questionable movie or having a drink, drop him immediately.

Are you culturally and socially compatible? Do you have similar interests? If so, you might want to consider pursuing the relationship and prayerfully seek God's will. Break off the courtship as soon as you discover that you are not either spiritually, mentally or socially agreeable. Do not allow yourself to get emotionally involved if you are not basically compatible. This would be very dangerous. Your emotions could lead you into an unwise marriage.

When I was showing interest in a girl my father would always ask, "Is she intelligent?"

"Of course in my lustful and rebellious years this was one of my least concerns. To be intelligent one must live reasonably by obeying God's Law. Girls should consider the question: Is this the man I want ruling over me? Will he lead the family wisely? Men should ponder this question: Is this the woman I want to be the mother of my children? Will she be of help or hindrance as I pursue my life's ambition and goals?

God provided what my father advised when he gave me Cindy as my wife. She is intelligent, virtuous, interesting, a good homemaker and a loving wife and mother.

"A virtuous woman who can find her? Her price is far above rubies." This saying is probably truer today than ever as thousands of American women have been brainwashed by the "women's liberation" propaganda.

When I speak out on campus against this modern philosophy, many of the girls become enraged. As they reach the boiling point I quickly add, "I'm not trying to put you women down, I'm just trying to put you in your proper place." This has brought me numerous punches and slaps over the years.

What is the proper place of a woman?

"And the Lord God said, It is not good that the man should be alone. I will make a help meet from him" (Genesis 2:18). First, the woman was created to be a help and companion to her husband. "Neither was the man created for the woman but the woman for man" (I Corinthians 11:9).

Secondly, the woman was intended to bare children and help

bring them up in the nurture and admonition of the Lord. "Unto the woman He said ... thou shalt bring forth children ..." (Genesis 3:16).

Even nature teaches us that the woman is to be a homemaker and the man is to earn a living. The mother carries the baby for nine months and becomes emotionally attached to it long before the father. The bond grows as she spends hours nursing the babe in the way God provided. It is impossible for the father to do this. God created him the stronger vessel so he could work to provide for his household. "But if any provide not for his own, and specially for those of his own house, he hath denied the faith and is worse than an infidel" (I Timothy 5:8).

The Woman's Place

God designed men to be the leaders and women to be their helpers. This should not anger the Christian woman because Jesus taught us all to take the attitude of a servant. But the women of this generation are selfish and they have been duped by the women libbers, many of whom are lesbians.

These contentious women try to convince others that they will be more fulfilled with their own career rather than being a good wife, mother and homemaker. They suggest a constant nine to five job for a cocktail-sipping executive would provide more joy than serving a God-fearing husband!

Many are asking: "Why be bored training and teaching your own children and watching them grow when you can drop them at the nursery? They will do all the work and you only have to see your little ones on the weekends."

The role of homemaker is belittled and made to look as though only a dumb, dull woman would want such a task. On the contrary, it takes great wisdom and intelligence to be a good wife and mother. It is a most honorable job and the rewards are great for those who do well.

The Word says: "Her children arise up and call her blessed; her husband also, and he praiseth her. Many daughters have done virtuously, but thou excellest them all. Give her the fruits of her hands; and let her own works praise her in the gates" (Proverbs 31:28, 29, 31).

After Eve sinned in the Garden of Eden God said to her, ". . . thy desire shall be unto thy husband and he shall rule over you" (Genesis 3:16).

I often say on campus that no matter how much she denies or fights it, every woman has a God-given desire to marry and bare children for a man who will lovingly rule over her.

After Eve's sin, God saw that since the woman is a more emotional being and more prone to be deceived by her sensibilities, she needs the leadership of a man who is governed by reason. As I have already mentioned, this is affirmed in the New Testament: "Wives submit yourselves unto your own husbands as unto the Lord. For the husband is the head of the wife even as Christ is the head of the church" (Ephesians 5:22, 23).

Despite her weaknesses the woman has had the honor bestowed upon her that can never be given any other creature of all God's creation. Independent of man, she had the exalted privilege of being the human instrumentality through whom Jesus Christ, God's only begotten Son, was born into the world. "Therefore the Lord himself shall give you a sign: Behold a virgin shall conceive and bear a son, and shall call his name Immanuel" (Isaiah 7:14). The word Immanuel means "God with us."

There are times in history when God puts a woman in a leadership position either because she is more suitable or because a man is not willing to do it. The latter was the case when God raised up Deborah the prophetess to be ruler and judge in Israel. The nation was so laden with sin that the men had become cowards and wimps. Phyllis Schafly, who almost single-handedly defeated the Equal Rights Amendment, is a good modern-day example of God using a woman in leadership.

In this day when the media is giving special attention to women, it is important that God-fearing women speak out for righteousness.

*There is scarce any expression
in Holy Writ which has given
more offense than this. The word
perfect is what many cannot bear.*
— *John Wesley*

15

ON CHRISTIAN PERFECTION

Since we preach so hard against sin, invariably I am asked the question a student addressed to me at the Indiana University, "Aren't you a sinner?"

"No, I am a saint. All Christians are saints," I replied.

"A saint! Well, just who made you a saint?" he asked.

"Jesus Christ," I answered.

"You mean you don't sin every day?" he insisted.

"No! Do you?" I replied.

"Everybody, including Christians sin daily in thought, word and deed," he said.

"You mean you cannot go a day without sinning?" I asked.

"No!" he said.

"A half day?" I asked.

"No!" he repeated.

"An hour? Do you suppose you could go for just one hour without sinning?" I asked.

"I don't see how," he replied.

"Five minutes, could you live five minutes without sinning?" I asked.

"I doubt it," he admitted.

"One minute, could you pass just one minute without sinning?" I asked.

"Oh, I suppose," he reluctantly responded.

"Aha! If you can go one minute without sinning, then you should be able to go five minutes. If you can pass five minutes, then you should be able to pass an hour. If you can experience an hour without sin, then you should be able to experience a day; if a day, then a week, if a week, then a month; if a month, a year. Finally friend, if you can live a year without sin then by the Spirit of God you can live above sin the rest of your life."

Angrily he responded, "Well, if you don't sin every day I don't see how you can call yourself a Christian." He turned and stomped off.

Bumper Sticker Religion

This student's problem was bad theology. He lacked knowledge of what the Bible teaches on holiness.

Romans 6:11 commands, "Reckon yourself to be dead indeed unto sin, but alive unto God through Jesus Christ our Lord."

The young man did not reckon or believe it so. We cannot experience beyond what our faith allows. The Word says: "As a man thinketh in his heart so is he." As long as a man thinks of himself as a sinner, he will sin because his thoughts become his actions. All of his struggles against sin are doomed for failure until he believes it possible to live holy by the power of the Spirit of God.

Regrettably, this man's attitude dominates modern "fundamental Christianity" today. It reflects what I call bumper sticker religion, "Christians are not perfect, just forgiven."

Be Ye Perfect

Yet Jesus said in the sermon on the mount, "Be ye therefore perfect even as your Father in heaven is perfect" (Matthew 5:48).

Does God command the impossible? If he did, that would make him a despot, a tyrant. But God is the Benevolent Moral Governor of the Universe. When he gives us a command, he provides a promise or the means to enable us to fulfill the command. Hebrews 10:14 gives us the means to perfection, "For by one offering (blood sacrifice) he hath perfected forever them that are sanctified." When one repents (forsakes sin) and puts his faith in the blood of Jesus Christ that cleanses from all sin, he is morally perfect.

Understand, our Lord commanded a moral or ethical perfection, not an absolute perfection. Only God is absolutely perfect. We are not perfect in knowledge and understanding. Therefore, we are susceptible to making mistakes. However, a mistake is not a sin. Sin is intentional transgression of the law; a mistake is an unintentional deviation from the truth or right conduct. If I intentionally misquoted a scripture to win an argument, it would be sinful. If I did it unintentionally because of imperfect memory, it would be a mistake.

A Christian may have faults. For example, he may worry too much; but only if his worries or even fears prevented him from doing the will of God, has he sinned.

Moral perfection is a purity of motives and intentions. "Blessed are the pure in heart for they shall see God" (Matthew 5:8).

Christian perfection is loving God with all of your heart, mind, soul and strength and loving your neighbor as yourself. On these two commandments hang all the law and the prophets. This is all that God requires of us.

God has given us the Bible that we might be "perfect" (I Timothy 3:17).

"These things I write unto you that you sin not" (I John 2:1), is another example of this truth.

Saved — From What?

"His name shall be called Jesus for he shall save his people from their sins" (Matthew 1:21), we are told in God's Word.

If a man still practices sin after claiming salvation, from what does he think he has been saved? Certainly not sin. Jesus did not come to save us in our sins but "from our sins."

When a man is saved, he will stop sinning. Jesus told the woman caught in adultery, "Go and sin no more." He did not say, "Go, sin a little bit every day." Nor did he say, "Of course I know you will sin, because my law is so hard and unreasonable, I don't really expect anyone to always obey."

SIN NO MORE! A Christian is one who has stopped sinning. A Christian obeys God. Listen to his Word: "And hereby we do know that we know him, if we keep his commandments. He that saith, I know him, and keepth not his commandments, is a liar, and the truth is not in him. But whoso keepth his word, in him verily is the love of God perfected" (I John 2:3-5). A Christian walks in the light he has with a right intention of heart.

"Whatsoever is born of God doth not commit sin; for his seed (God's word) remaineth in him: and he cannot sin, because he is born of God" (I John 3:9), is another example of this truth.

The born again man cannot sin. Studying the context of the verse above, we understand it to mean that the Christian is able not to sin. Not that he is unable to sin. The honest man can steal but if he steals he is no longer an honest man. The truthful man can lie but if he lies he is no longer a truthful man. The pure man can lust but if he lusts he is no longer a pure man. The Christian can sin but if he does he no longer has Biblical grounds to consider himself a Christian.

It is like George Washington saying to his father, "Father, I cannot tell a lie, I cut down the cherry tree." What was George saying? "Father, I am your son. I can't lie. There is the family name to consider." So it is with the Christian. We are sons of God. God is our Father. We are called Christians. We have the family name to consider. How can we call ourselves Christians and lie, steal, cheat, lust or be intemperate, etc. God forbid that we should sin! We refuse to sin. We hate sin. We love God. We love his law.

Sin is the result of a lack of love for God and our neighbors. It is choosing to put self ahead of God and our fellows. "Loving God means doing what he tells us to do, and really, that isn't hard at all" (I John 5:3 L.B.). Sin is the result of lack of faith in God to deliver us from evil.

The Great Escape

We are taught in the Word: "There hath no temptation taken you but such as is common to man: but God is faithful, who will not suffer you to be tempted above that ye are able; but will with the temptation also make a way to escape, that ye may be able to bear it" (I Corinthians 10:13).

One is tempted to lie. What is the way to escape? Simply tell the truth. You are tempted to cheat. Be honest. You are tempted to lust. Think about what is pure and holy. The battleground is the mind. Temptation only becomes sin if you should submit your will to the evil thought. "Submit yourself to God. Resist the devil and he will flee from you" (James 4:7). Do not make your sin greater than God.

Pleading For Sin

Hearing this truth, the hypocrite, in desperation, appeals to the Word of God to justify his sin. "What about I John 1:8? "If we say we have no sin we deceive ourselves, and the truth is not in us." Certainly, this verse taken out of context would contradict the teaching of Christian perfection.

Therefore, let us consider verse eight in the context of the book. Remember John's purpose in writing I John: "These things I write unto that you sin not" (2:1). If it is impossible not to sin, then John's purpose is vain. Look at verse six of chapter one. "If we say we have fellowship with Jesus Christ, and walk in darkness, we lie, and do not the truth." Verses six and eight are both talking about liars, people who say they are Christians (have fellowship) yet continue to sin (walk in darkness), are liars because they don't obey (do) the truth. "But if we walk in the light, as he is in the light, we have fellowship one with another, and the blood of Jesus Christ his Son cleanseth us from all sin" (Verse 7).

Christianity is a walk; the new birth is merely the first step. At the new birth we step out of Satan's kingdom into God's Kingdom. We step out of darkness (sin) into the light (righteousness). "If ye continue in my word, then are ye my disciples indeed; and ye shall know the truth, and the truth shall make you free" (John 8:31, 32). If we do the truth, or are doers and not just hearers of the Word, then we shall be free. Free from what? Sin! "Whosoever committeth sin is the slave of sin" (John 8:34). Praise God! He has set us free from sin. "Being then made free from sin, we have become the servants of righteousness" (Romans 6:18).

"He that committeth sin is of the devil" (I John 3:8).

Saint or Sinner?

A Christian serves God and righteousness. An unbeliever serves sin and Satan. No man can serve two masters. You are either a saint or sinner.

Now we are prepared to understand verse eight. The verse that the self-righteous love to claim is: "If we say we have no sin, we deceive ourselves, and the truth is not in us." There are many professing Christians who say that they have no sin for which God will hold them accountable; that their sins are covered by the blood of Jesus. Yet, by their own testimony, they sin daily in thought, word and deed. They are deceived. They say God does not see their sin. "All God sees is the blood. All God sees is Jesus in our hearts," they say. What, do they think that the precious blood is ineffectual; that there is no power in the blood? The blood of bulls and goats only covered sin, but "the blood of Jesus Christ his Son cleanseth us from all sin," not some, not most, but all sin. God does not leave behind a few secret sins for man to indulge.

Oh! the lengths that men will go to excuse their sins. God is not blind; he will judge sin. Sin always condemns whether the sinner professes to believe in Jesus. The truth is not in these hypocrites. Their own words witness against them. If the truth were in them, they would obey the commandments of the Lord, they would obey his Word, they would walk as Jesus walked (I John 2:4, 5).

Verse nine says: "If we confess our sins, he is faithful and just to forgive us our sins, and to cleanse us from all unrighteousness." Notice the big little word if. Biblical confession of sins always implies repentance which means forsaking the sin. When God forgives, he cleanses. The two go hand in hand. If there is no cleansing, there has been no forgiveness. If there is no forgiveness, it is because there has been no true confession (repentance). "Ye know that Jesus was manifested to take away our sin" (I John 3:6). You cannot hold onto your sins and hold onto the SAVIOUR.

Verse 10 says: "If we say we have not sinned, we make him a liar, and his word is not in us" Hearken unto the tense — past tense. "All have sinned" (Romans 3:23). Make sure your sins are in the past. We Christians know that "whosoever is born of God, sinneth not" (I John 5:15). Continue in his Word, not in sin. "Walk in the spirit and ye shall not fulfill the lust of the flesh" (Galatians 5:16).

"We know that everyone that doeth righteousness is born of him" (John 2:29). These are religious liars who claim they can continue to sin and be his disciples. But, his Word is in us and it keeps us holy. Sin NO MORE.

Grace Works

Gainsayers will cry, "You are preaching salvation through works, instead of by grace."

Salvation is by grace through faith. Grace is the cause of our salvation, faith is the means by which we obtain grace and works of obedience are the effect or evidence of our salvation. "For the grace of God that bringeth salvation hath appeared to all men, teaching us that, denying ungodliness and worldly lust, we should live soberly, righteously, and godly, in this present world" (Titus 2:11, 12). The same grace that pardons our sin delivers us from sin and keeps us from sin. "For sin shall not have dominion over you: for ye are not under the law, but under grace" (Romans 6:14).

Reader, if sin still has control over you "causing" you to sin daily then you are not under grace but have a legalistic relationship with God. If you are under grace then this power has freed you from sin to become a servant of righteousness. "What then? Shall we sin, because we are not under the law, but under grace? GOD FORBID" (Romans 6:15). Never use grace to excuse your sin. Christian liberty is not the freedom to do as we please but to do as we ought — obey God. By God's grace through faith we are now free to obey God and to not sin anymore. Grace will always produce works of righteousness. Where there is no obedience there has been no work of grace.

An Important Distinction

There is much confusion on the subject of perfection because of a failure to make a proper distinction between purity and maturity. Perfection refers to purity. When a man is born again he is as perfect as he is ever going to be but certainly he is not mature. The rosebud is just as perfect as the full-blown rose. There is a definite sense in which we are being sanctified or growing in grace (maturing). I make no claims to be a full-blown rose yet; neither am I still a rosebud!

Perfection, sanctification or holiness (these terms are generally used interchangeably in the scriptures) are not a gradual putting off of sin because forsaking all sin is a condition to being born again. Christian perfection is a total submission to all light we possess at a given moment. As the Holy Spirit progressively reveals the character of God and our moral obligation, the Christian is responsible to conform to this greater understanding. There may be occasional transgressions or brief lapses into sin in the life of a saint but as he grows in grace and knowledge such incidents will be less likely. He will reach a point where sin virtually does not take place in his life and he will have become a father of the faith.

Benediction

"And the God of peace sanctify you wholly; and I pray God your whole spirit and soul and body be preserved blameless unto the coming of our Lord Jesus Christ. Faithful is he that calleth you, who also will do it" (I Thessalonians 5:23).

*The people that do know their
God shall be strong, and do exploits!*
— Daniel 11:32

16

SAINTS OF VALOR

"Mama, you've got to come down on campus and hear this man preach; the students can handle everything but the truth."

Mrs. Pat Noordewier listened skeptically as her son Tommy described my ministry and the student response at the University of Wisconsin. Then he handed her a copy of my testimony tract "From Death to Life." When Mrs. Noordewier saw the top picture of me as a hippie freak she decided to go to campus and make sure I was not a guru. She insisted her husband Mick take off work early and they both hurried to the scene.

Witnessing The Campus Ministry first hand, Mrs. Noordewier exclaimed, "This must be the way Jesus did it." That evening the Noordewiers took me to dinner and I was able to explain my purpose and methods. They asked if there was anything they could do to help. I told them that Sister Cindy and a companion would be coming through town in a few weeks and if they could give them lodging it would be a big help. They agreed.

The Noordewiers soon became some of our best supporters. Mrs. Noordewier started making most of Sister Cindy's clothes. When any of the campus preachers came to town they were welcomed at the Noordewiers! They often helped with our car expenses and even gave us love offerings to send us to the next city. This, coupled with their friendship, was a great blessing. But we did not realize that God had an even greater purpose in introducing us to the Noordewiers: he was going to raise up another campus preacher.

Sister Pat

From the beginning Mrs. Noordewier would join us on campus and pray for the students as we preached to them. We recognized that she had a great zeal for the lost but we were ignorant of her burning desire to preach the Gospel.

In the fall of 1981 Sister Cindy and Mrs. Noordewier journeyed to her alma matar, the University of Arkansas. Sister Cindy had been preaching to a huge crowd for several hours and she needed a break. She told the students that she was going inside for a few minutes but if they had any questions Mrs. Noordewier would answer them.

To their surprise the whole crowd surrounded her and began asking questions. She spent two hours giving a reason for the faith that is within her.

This was the beginning of "Sister Pat" and her ministry to college students. The following spring she joined Sister Cindy on campuses in Arkansas, Oklahoma, New Mexico and Colorado.

Sister Pat returned to Madison with a burden to preach at the University of Wisconsin. Mick gave his blessing and she started preaching there regularly — and immediately gained attention on campus. Not only is Sister Pat anointed of God to preach but she has a natural talent for silencing the hecklers and answering trick questions.

One day as Cindy preached, the crowd grew exceptionally rowdy. She retreated inside and answered questions. When she returned Sister Pat had the crowd calmed and listening.

Sister Cindy later asked her how she did it.

She responded, "I'm experienced, I raised three children of my own."

Some might suggest that college students could not relate to a grandmother but Sister Pat's age gives her more credibility and demands respect. The students look at her as a mother image. In this generation of rebellious women the youth need such a godly example.   .

Although Pat always led a conservative and outwardly moral life, she was not always a godly example. The Noordewiers were the typical affluent American family. Mick worked his way to a top administrative position in the U.S. Forest Service. He was a good husband and father. Pat was a capable wife and mother; a companion to her husband and instructor to her children. For years the Noordewiers were Presbyterians. Mick was a deacon in the church and Pat was a Sunday school teacher. Nevertheless, they were selfish, lost and hell-bound.

In 1972 Sister Pat went with her sister to a Pentecostal Church meeting in Little Rock, Arkansas. That night Pat was wonderfully saved and filled with the Holy Spirit. She rushed home and told her husband the exciting news. Mick began to seek God more and eventually was converted. Pat immediately had two great desires: one, thoroughly study the scriptures; two, win the whole world to Christ. Each day after Mick went to the office she quickly did the house work and then spent hours studying and reading the Bible. God was preparing her for The Campus Ministry.

Today, Sister Pat is a regular fixture in the free speech mall at the University of Wisconsin. She also makes fall and spring tours to the state's many other universities and colleges. In addition, she takes a couple of trips a year with Sister Cindy and me. Mick is very supportive of her work and The Campus Ministry.

Bobby Bible and The Christian Brothers

When I started preaching on campus "Holy Hubert" Lindsey was the only other person I knew who ministered in this way. Later, I met Bob Engle (Bobby Bible), Harvey Baldwin (Jeremiah Christian) and Paul Mitchell who started a preaching ministry on campus about the same time as "Holy Hubert." They call themselves the "Christian Brothers" and parade on campus raising high banners which read TURN OR BURN, READ THE BIBLE BEFORE IT'S TOO LATE, and JESUS SAVES FROM HELL. These colorful, well-designed signs quickly draw the attention of a crowd. They carry on throughout the afternoon preaching a strong message on judgment.

While many campus preachers have come and gone over the years the "Christian Brothers" remain steadfast in their calling headquartering out of Long Beach, California. They concentrate their efforts on the West Coast but also take tours into the East.

They have trained other young men to follow in their footsteps so that especially in Southern California you will likely see these banner-carrying brothers battling the hosts of hell, not only on the campuses but at parades, the Grand Prix, beaches, demonstrations and rock concerts.

Frequently, they travel far and wide to attend ministers' conferences and Christian Conventions to challenge the lukewarm to rise up against evil and reach out to the lost in public places.

The "Christian Brothers" are true soldiers of the Cross who refuse to compromise with the world or the devil.

Bro Cope

In the fall of 1977 Max Lynch and I were making a tour of eastern campuses and stopped at Penn State University. At the end of the day Bro Cope, a man in his late 20s, introduced himself to us. He had been a radical in the 60s who had graduated from Penn State several years earlier. After his conversion Bro returned to his alma mater having said to God, "Lord, I'll do anything you want me to do but don't make me preach." But by Easter 1977 Bro was preaching to crowds of several hundred in front of Willard Hall.

God directed him not to get a job so that he could devote himself to working full-time on the campus to promote revival. The first year he had to live in his car through a cold Pennsylvania winter. Miraculously the Lord provided food for him. On one winter day Bro walked by a restaurant and found a hot meat loaf sandwich wrapped on the window sill. No one was in sight on the street. Even though he only had an income of $880 his first year, all of his needs were supplied without taking government relief or asking anyone for money or any other help.

Bro and his associate, Steve Michaels, had worked hard to break up the fallow ground and prepare the students' hearts for our message. On several return visits to Penn State I worked and fellowshipped closely with these brethren. Each year I would encourage Bro to travel the southern states with me in the winter. Finally, in February 1982, God released Bro to accompany me for six weeks. He returned to Penn State with a renewed vision. Bro wanted to be on the road more in 1982-83 but he did not have suitable transportation. Therefore, he prayed that God would give him a good car. In order to answer his prayer the Lord moved the Fortress Church in Lawrenceville, Georgia, to give me a generous downpayment on a new Chrysler New Yorker. Then the Lord led me to give my Chrysler Cordoba to Bro. Since getting his car Bro has been traveling the winter months.

Early in 1983 Bro and I were ministering at UCLA. Bro was preaching to the Jews, "You are stiff-necked and hard-hearted, and are always resisting the Holy Spirit."

Suddenly two Jews ran up to the podium to attack him but Bro faced them down as he plunged in the sword even deeper, cutting to the quick.

One of them threatened, "If you didn't have glasses on I

would punch you in the mouth."

Bro obliged him by removing his glasses and thrusting out his chin to make an easier target and the man backed down.

The next day Bro waxed bolder and repeatedly commanded the crowd, "Repent now, in the name of Jesus. Fall to you knees on the grass and repent." He kept this up for several minutes.

A young man approached Bro. "What do you want?" Bro asked, assuming him to be another mocker.

"I want to get saved," he replied. He knelt in front of 120 people and repented.

Bro turned the crowd over to me and he began to minister to the new convert. Meanwhile, a girl approached Bro and confessed that she had been a Christian but had turned to fornication, partying and drunkenness. When the young man had knelt down, she was so convicted that she also repented.

Later, when Bro was preaching again, one of the Jews who had tried to attack him the previous day came up to me to talk. I asked him if he wanted to get saved. He said, "Yes." Right after he prayed, he came forward to testify to the crowd of his conversion. Since there were so many Jewish infidels in the crowd, he was immediately besieged by these zealots. He continued to testify of how he felt changed.

In the spring of 1984 Bro preached at Texas Tech University in Lubbock where he encountered extreme difficulty with wimpy religionists. One fellow stood most of the day listening intently and observing the furor surrounding the preaching of the Gospel. Towards the end of the day he asked to address the crowd. He chided them saying, "You have been trying to discredit this evangelist all day but have been unable. He has completely destroyed every objection you people have raised."

Naturally, Bro thought the man to be a Christian. Finally, as Bro was preparing to leave, he asked, "Are there any more questions?"

Bro's defender quickly said, "Yes, where do we go from here?"

"Are you a Christian?" Bro asked.

"No."

"Would you like to be?"

"Yes."

Bro began to tell him of the extreme cost of following Jesus in terms of total commitment, holy living and persecution. Try as he did, Bro was not able to dissuade him from getting saved. Bro turned him over to a pastor — a man he was working with — for more ministry. The pastor spent several hours telling him of the cost. He could not dissuade him from salvation (not that they did not want him to be saved but that they wanted an informed convert).

Finally, the young man said, "Look, if Jesus tells me tomorrow to go to Africa, I am ready to obey him." They thought he was surely ready. He lit up like a Roman candle as soon as he prayed for salvation. Today he is going strong in the faith in Lubbock.

When Bro is not on the road he continues his ministry at Penn State. So many young men have followed Bro's example at Penn State that there is somewhat of a problem as to who will speak when. Several that Bro trained are in preaching ministeries across the country. Bro contends zealously for the perfection of the saints and has suffered much for the cause of Christ.

Be ye followers of me,
even as I also am of Christ.
— I Corinthians 1:11

17

FOLLOW-UP?

What about follow-up? Our ministry has sometimes been criticized because we do not emphasize a follow-up program for students.

Jesus and the apostles did not consider follow-up vital to successful evangelism. Instead, Jesus expected true disciples to follow him. When he witnessed to Peter and Andrew, he said, "Follow me, and I will make you fishers of men." He expected them to make an immediate decision to change the whole direction of their lives.

When the rich young ruler eagerly asked, "What good thing shall I do, that I may have eternal life?" Jesus did not take this wonderful opportunity to lecture him on the doctrine that salvation is not of works but of grace. Nor did he preach on his upcoming death and resurrection. First, he preached the law. When the man claimed to have kept it, Jesus demanded proof, "If thou wilt be perfect, go and sell that thou hast, and give to the poor, and thou shalt have treasure in heaven: and come and

FOLLOW ME."

When the man heard the cost of discipleship, he quickly lost interest in the salvation of his soul and he left saddened because he had great wealth with which he could not part. Notice that Jesus did not go chasing after him or plead with him to hear more. He did use the incident to impress upon his disciples the necessity of total commitment: "Every one that hath forsaken houses, or brethren, or sisters, or father, or mother, or wife, or children, or lands, for my name sake, shall receive an hundredfold, and shall inherit everlasting life" (Matthew 19:29).

Jesus did not gradually reveal his expectations to the interested seeker but instead demanded an immediate consecration to the Kingdom of all a man's possessions and ambitions. Follow-up program? No, just a straightforward challenge to either follow after the riches and joys of heaven, or continue to set your affections on the things of this life on earth. Jesus expected converts to have as little desire for this world as a dead person has. Another time when Jesus was walking along the way with his disciples a fervent youth said, "Lord, I will follow thee withersoever thou goest."

And Jesus answered him, "Foxes have holes, and birds of the air have nests; but the Son of man hath not where to lay his head" (Luke 9:57, 58). There was no attempt to baptize, no invitation to further Bible study, no explanation of the need for Christian fellowship, no promise of a wonderful plan, no encouragement — but a reminder to count the cost.

And Jesus said unto another, "Follow me."
But he said, "Lord, suffer me first to go and bury my father."

Jesus answered, "Let the dead bury the dead; but go thou and preach the Kingdom of God" (Luke 9:59, 60). No "me first" attitude for a true believer; it must be the Kingdom of God first. No excuses accepted by the Lord — he expected instant obedience. Go and preach a life-giving message.

Following Jesus' Example

When the demonic of the Gadarenes, out of whom Jesus cast a legion of devils, wanted to stay with him, Jesus would not let him do it, but said, "Go home to your friends, and tell them how great things the Lord hath done for thee" (Mark 5:19).

When Jesus exposed the adultery of the woman at the well, she went into town telling everybody about Jesus and brought them out to hear more. Her conversion sparked a great revival.

If a man has been truly converted one of the first things he will want to do is tell others. Charles Finney said, "Seest thou a professed convert to Christ whose compassions are not stirred, and whose zeal for the salvation of souls is not awakened? Be assured that you behold a hypocrite."

I am not denying that there are principles of follow-up found in the Bible. Jesus not only ministered to the lost but spent a considerable amount of time training his 12 disciples to follow him and continue his work. For four years Cindy followed about two weeks behind me on the college circuit to water the seed which I had sown. Occasionally, she was even able to harvest.

In December 1980 at Florida State University I was daily heckled by a very persistent fellow. It is ironic that the students who try to shout me down insist I leave campus and say my preaching is nonsense, will skip classes and spend hours listening to me.

Sister Cindy followed up my ministry at Florida State and this same heckler told her he had become interested in Bible prophecy. He asked her many questions but insisted he was not open to this "Jesus stuff." Sister Cindy, believing that he would be converted, asked a Christian student to keep an eye on him. When she returned to FSU with "Holy Hubert" in April, they were greeted by the smiling face of the one "who persecuted us in times past, but now preached the faith which he once destroyed." They glorified God in him. This former heckler said he looked forward to preaching to his fellow students. Sister

Cindy told him that this was his day. After drawing the crowd she called on him to give his testimony.

As he spoke he confessed that he had been one of the worst mockers on campus. He admitted that after several days of scorning he began to ask himself why he kept going back to listen. He said that he realized that the truth we spoke was what upset him but at the same time drew him back. He told the students, "Some of you probably remember me, I was a big mouth for the devil, but today I'm a big mouth for Jesus." This man graduated, married and became a missionary to Mexico. To my knowledge he is still working for the Lord there.

The Lord had me in a full-time ministry within weeks after my conversion. He sent me to the streets, nursing homes, jails, hospitals, homes and into the public schools to infiltrate and do undercover work as a substitute teacher. Within six months I started a weekly Bible study in an old school house. Within a year I conducted a two-week church revival. Within two years I was full-time in The Campus Ministry.

Sister Cindy moved even more quickly. Within a month after being saved she was giving her testimony on the colleges with Max and me. Ten weeks after her conversion she was preaching weekly at the University of Florida. After six months she forsook a journalism career and started traveling the campuses full-time with Max and me. Cindy would stay in a Christian home at night and meet us daily on campus. After nine months she was making the campus circuit via Greyhound buses on her own.

Our examples should not be considered the exception. When there has been a total surrender on the part of the new convert, and with proper encouragement from Christian leadership, examples such as ours can become the rule. Actually, most new-born Christians have great zeal to be active in the ministry. However, the cares of this world, or the deceitfulness of riches may soon cool their ardor. Of course, the backsliders are also ever present to throw a wet blanket on them to put out their fire.

Follow Us

Paul said, "Be ye followers of me, even as I also am of Christ" (I Corinthians 11:1). Paul was not ashamed to set himself up as an example of what a Christian ought to do and be. For too long we have set up the apostles as unique men who lived the Christian life on a higher plane than we could ever hope to attain. Not so. They, like us, were mere men subject to like passions as we are.

I will never forget the memorable words my pastor, Clyde Swalls, said to me shortly after my conversion: "Jed, do you realize that the same Spirit that dwelled in the Apostle Paul dwells in you? Therefore, whatever he accomplished you can do also; even a greater ministry is available to you. For it is not by human might, or power, but by the Spirit that we do great works for God."

From that moment I was determined to be a twentieth-century Paul. Believers today have set their goals too low. Pastors expect so little and challenge their congregation so weakly that the typical attitude is "How much can I get away with and still make it to heaven?"

Where are the fishers of men? Where are the ark builders, the sword fighters, the giant slayers, the sun stoppers, the mountain climbers, the nation movers and the martyrs?

The Bible Institutes and Christian Liberal Arts Colleges, with a few exceptions, are not much better than the state universities. The vast majority of students, after two to four years of training, grow soft, complacent, comfortable and remain surprisingly ignorant of the Bible and sound theology. I would match the biblical knowledge, theological understanding and general wisdom of Jim Gilles, Pat Noordewier and Sister Cindy (three of whom I have had the privilege of training) against any Bible college or seminary graduate. While the student has been wilting in the classroom Brother Jim, Sister Pat and Sister Cindy have been out in the field battling the forces of evil and diligently studying the Bible and the works of the great theologians such as Charles Finney — and learning to be individuals of prayer by interceding daily on behalf of those they are preaching to. Not only have they been reaching the lost but church doors have opened to enable them to minister to the saints. There is no substitute for on-the-job training.

Follow up? Most people to whom I preach I may never see again. But there have been surprises.

When I first went to Southern Oregon College in Ashland a young man was already preaching. He told me he had been converted in a hotel meeting which I had held in Tucson, Arizona several years ago. Interestingly enough, there were only four people in the service. I preached from Psalms 94:16: "Who will rise up?" They all volunteered. When this preacher started his work at Southern Oregon he had trouble with the authorities but defended his rights, paving the way for our ministry.

Rich Rife was also a volunteer at the meeting in Tucson and he now preaches on the streets of America's largest cities. They had followed me up!

At the University of Iowa I was preaching in the Old Capital area close to a city bus stop. Ron Alberts, a bus driver, stopped there regularly to pick up students and listened to my message as his passengers boarded. Immediately after work he would rush down to campus and hear me preach the rest of the day. I was speaking nightly to Grace Fellowship which met in the Wesley Foundation. Ron started attending these meetings and one night committed his life to Christ. The next year Ron followed me for several weeks on the campuses, during which he became bold to share the Gospel. When he returned to Iowa City he was a more effective witness on his bus route.

The student population is very transient. Therefore, it is not unusual for them to hear me on different campuses. There is an old adage: "Throw a shoe into a pack of dogs, and the only one who yelps is the one who gets hit."

One day at the University of Colorado one of the dogs decided to throw back. He used snowballs which I had to — sometimes unsuccessfully — dodge.

The next year at the University of Texas I witnessed to a

student and eventually led him in a prayer of repentance and faith. He then confessed that he had transferred from the University of Colorado and that he was the one who had thrown snowballs at me the year before. The following year when I returned to UT, he had become an active member in the Maranatha Christian Church. By the next year he had become a pastor in the church!

There are certain campuses where we preach annually and are therefore able to do some follow-up. We have often discovered that we have great effect on the students even though our ministry may not result in their immediate conversion. At the end of each school year I have heard testimonies from students that go much like this one from a student at the University of California at San Diego:

"Brother Jed, I want to shake your hand. I have heard you speak every year since I was a freshman. I graduate this year so I will probably never hear you again. Therefore, I wanted to let you know that your annual ministry to this campus has been one of the highlights of my education. You are the most powerful speaker I have ever heard. I am not a Christian, but I have thought a lot about what you say. You have taught me most of what I know about the Bible and I have learned a lot. Thank you for coming to this campus."

Obviously, such remarks at the end of a long year of evangelism are a great encouragement to me.

In the late 70s a dirty old man who called himself "The Swami" came to the UCLA free-speech area to tell obscene stories. He started competing for the attention of the crowd that had gathered to listen to me. He made such a commotion that it was very difficult to get my message across, so I moved to another area. At first only a few pursued me. Most of these were Christians, but at least one girl was not; and she made serious inquiry into the nature of salvation. Within 15 minutes four Christians and I knelt and prayed with the girl for the salvation of her soul. Meanwhile, the crowd grew bored with the "The

Swami," and returned to hear me preach. I never saw the girl again but in 1983 a Christian student reminded me of the conversion and informed me that she had graduated and was a missionary in South America. Incidents like this have confirmed to me that a follow-up program, although helpful, is not necessary.

Follow-Up Fallacy

The over-emphasis on a follow-up ministry is a result of offering salvation without repentance. Jesus' first public message was "Repent ye, and believe the gospel" (Mark 1:15). His last words to his disciples before ascending into heaven included the exhortation "That repentance and remission of sins should be preached in his name among all nations, beginning at Jerusalem" (Luke 24:47).

Peter preached to a crowd of Jews that gathered at the temple gate after he healed the lame man: "Repent ye therefore, and be converted, that your sins may be blotted out" (Acts 20:21). Repentance and faith are both prerequisites for salvation.

Most evangelism today says: "Only believe," or "Jesus will accept you just as you are" or "Just ask Jesus into your heart," or "Accept him as your personal Saviour."

If anything is said of repentance, it comes later. No wonder they must have elaborate follow-up programs. Under this plan how could anyone get saved from sin? The biblical order is REPENT AND BELIEVE, Not believe and repent. The fact of the matter is that without repentance there is no saving faith.

If there has been true repentance and faith, we will not have to beg and plead for the individual to come to Bible studies or church. If he is a Christian he will study to show himself approved. He will not desire to forsake the gathering together of his brethren. If he has been born again, we will not have to cajole him to give up drinking, swearing or any other sin. Indeed, if he is a true convert, he has forsaken sin. We do not have to exhort him to be unselfish. If he is a Christian, his life is centered in God and in services to his fellow man.

Many have been deceived into believing that they may know Jesus as their personal Saviour without recognizing him as Lord. Such people are not following Jesus in truth. The fact of the matter is that Jesus does not become a man's Saviour until he is recognized as Lord in every area of life. The Word says: "That if thou shalt confess with thy mouth the Lord Jesus, and shalt believe in thine heart that God has raised him from the dead, thou shalt be saved" (Romans 10:9).

If he is not Lord of all then he is not Lord at all.

What is the evidence that a man believes in his heart? Many have made mere mental assent to certain fundamental facts concerning Jesus Christ but do not believe in their hearts. If a man believes in his heart, he will obey. Obedience is the evidence of faith. The Bible says: "For with the heart man believeth unto righteousness; and with the mouth confession is made unto salvation" (Romans 10:10). Faith from the heart will produce a righteous life. According to God's Word: "Ye know that every one that doeth righteousness is born of Jesus Christ" (I John 2:29).

Evangelicals, in their zeal to encourage individuals to be saved, too often lead a man into a premature confession with his mouth when there has been no work of repentance in the heart. If Christendom had more John the Baptists warning the multitude, "Oh generation of vipers, who hath warned you to flee from the wrath to come? Bring forth therefore fruits worthy of repentance" (Luke 3:7, 8), a follow-up program would not be necessary.

The only kind of Christianity I see in the Bible is total commitment. One must forsake all: the world, the flesh and the devil in order to qualify to be a Christian and remain one. This is the only Christianity I know to preach. Until this message is sounded loudly and clearly from the pulpit, follow-up will be a constant concern in Christendom.

There are not two kinds of Christians: the few that are fully committed and the many that are only partially committed. This must be understood or evangelicals are forever condemned to a life of cajoling, coaxing, and pleading, instead of patiently correcting, instructing and inspiring in both doctrine and practice.

Plowing and Planting

One plants the seed, another may water it. But it is God that gives the increase. Our ministry is primarily one of plowing and planting. Regrettably, there are too many who are trying to plant without first plowing the field. One seed that became a beautiful flower sent me a thank-you note:

> Dear Jed,
> I want to thank you so very much for coming to speak at Ohio University. I've been at O.U. for three years and heard you speak each time. I listened the first two years, but this year was different. O.U. has had other evangelists come, but the people really listen to what you're saying because you truly love God and show this love towards others. You probably don't remember me, but after one of your "teachings" on the college green you were speaking to a girl and her boyfriend. You really helped her. Then you spoke to me on Eastern Religions. After you left my friend and I had some discussions on God and Religions. Since then I've quit going to Hare Kishna suppers, and have cut ties with them totally. I just want to thank you for planting the seeds and helping me realize how true God is.
> May God be with you.
> Love in Him,
> Susan W.

We are always anxious to work with Christians, both on campus and in local churches, who are willing to water the seed which we have sown. Rev. Bob Rodgers, when he pastored Calvary Assembly in Lexington, Kentucky, testified that 50 students started attending his church as a result of my daily meetings on campus and nightly meetings in his church which was just a few blocks away.

The students who manned the Intervarsity book table at UCLA informed me that they had distributed more literature in the few days I had been on campus than they had all year.

Many students in Campus Crusade for Christ have told me that after I have preached on campus the students are much more open to discussion. They say that when I am ministering, students make more appointments for personal interviews than at any other time of the year. If we get a convert to Christ, we attempt to introduce him to someone we know to be a Christian. However, if there has been a true conversion, we are confident that the new Christian will seek out fellowship.

Our ministry is so much more effective when the Christian leadership on campus fully supports and cooperates with our efforts. Such was the case at Montana State University in March 1984.

We blew into Bozeman, Montana, with a heavy snow storm. When we started preaching it was snowing so hard we could barely see. The Word of God soon froze about 200 students in their tracks. Despite the cold elements, a FIRE was kindled that would not be put out.

Initially at Montana State it seemed we were as unwanted as the spring snow. I stabbed the students with the Sword of the Spirit for four hours and by late afternoon they were as angry and unreasonable as wounded animals.

I went into the cafeteria for a hot drink and over 50 students followed me. Most attempted to justify their rebellion against God by asking questions with the same attitude the Pharisees confronted Jesus. It seemed like your typical campus of apathetic sinners, lukewarm and ignorant professing Christians and maybe a few Lots. We returned with the snow the next day and again preached outdoors to huge crowds for several hours. When it seemed they might gnash me with their teeth, I advanced to the cafeteria. This time 100 students followed me.

Many of them swarmed around Sister Cindy who was already inside with a Chi Alpha (Assembly of God) minister, John Engels, who described the scene:

"One afternoon when I was talking with Cindy in the Student Union Building's Coffee Shop, the crowd Jed was speaking to outside followed him inside. Before I knew it, about 50-100 students had crowded around us asking many questions. I had never preached the Gospel in this way before. Imagine, sitting at a table with coffee, preaching to the multitudes! It wasn't very long until we were all asked to leave the coffee shop because of all the commotion. We then went with about 75 people to a lounge and shared the gospel for another two hours there."

This was our first sign of breakthrough.

That evening John Engels and the Intervarsity Christian Fellowship minister took us to dinner. I reasoned with them on holiness, righteousness and confrontation evangelism for two and one-half hours. The two leaders felt other Christians on campus needed to hear my message so they called a special indoor meeting the next night.

Over 100 came to the service including a MSU professor and his prayer group. I exhorted them to holy living and good works and "God's word went forth and melted them" (Psalms 147:18). Conviction seized the crowd and about 30 stood and confessed their sins including lust, lukewarmness and fighting our ministry. Many committed themselves to pray and to stand for righteousness until their university saw true revival!

John Engels concluded:

"Jed and Cindy Smock's challenge to Holy Living stirred much controversy among Christians, but it was exciting to see God melt hearts and do significant things in the lives of us. Holiness has been the catchword since they came."

The following is a letter from one revived Montana State student:

Dear Brother Jed and Sister Cindy,
   I praise God for your marvelous ministry!
   Thank you for coming to MSU this spring. I must

confess that when I first heard you speaking I didn't know what to think, but by the third day I could learn to appreciate your unique methods of evangelism.

I believe the Gospel you are presenting is the Gospel for us in the U.S. today. We've heard that God loves us, and it's time we hear how God sees our sin. You are absolutely right about the moral behavior of college students today. It's time they are told that sin is not O.K., and that there are standards by which we will all someday be judged.

Your time spent on our campus encouraged many of us to be more vocal Christians and stand up for our beliefs. I found numerous opportunities open up for witnessing. God was the talk of the campus for a change. A fellow student testified at a Bible study how because of your ministry he broke up a fight between drunken fraternity boys and witnessed to them about Christ for two hours. One student came to the Lord as a result. Praise God!

In my opinion you two were the biggest thing that ever came to MSU, much more of an impact than anything in my experience. I was and am really amazed at the powerful inspired influence you had. I don't know how you put up with the disgusting hassles you receive. It is certainly the work of the Holy Spirit . . .

Bill Keightley — MSU History major

*Man will ultimately be
governed by God or by tyrants.*
— Benjamin Franklin

18

MORE ISSUES
AND ANSWERS

Martin Luther said that if a man preaches without addressing the issue of the day, he has not preached the Gospel. Why? Because God has a standard for every realm of life. There is a Christian economics, a Christian government, a Christian education and a Christian family. God is not just ruler over Sunday church services. Students constantly confront us with the controversies of the day and we are ready to give them the biblical position. Separation of church and state, capitalism versus socialism and capital punishment are three issues we are commonly confronted with.

Separation of Church and State

"You've got no right to be on this campus. Haven't you heard, the Constitution says, 'separation of church and state?' " a student shouts from the crowd.

"The expression, separation of church and state is not found in the United States Constitution," I reply. "The first amendment states, 'Congress shall make no law respecting an establishment of religion, or prohibiting the free exercise thereof . . .' There is no other mention of religion or any reference to the church in the Constitution. Notice the amendment says freedom of religion, not freedom from religion."

Separation of church and state was a concern of our Founding Fathers but in a much different sense than it has been advocated since the 1950s by the Supreme Court. The founders never intended government to be divorced from God and his rule over the affairs of men. Their primary concern in the establishment clause was to protect the church from the encroachment of the federal government. Most of them or their fathers had come over from England where to this day there is an established tax-supported state church. They feared a national denominational church, a "Church of America," such as the Anglican Church of England.

The signers of the Declaration of Independence appealed to "the laws of nature and of nature's God, the Supreme Judge of the world" to justify the United Colonies in proclaiming separation from Great Britian.

Note the cherished words: "We hold these truths to be self-evident that all men are created equal; that they are endowed by their CREATOR with certain unalienable rights . . ."

These noble men recognized that it was God who determined human rights and these liberties cannot be taken away or transferred to another.

In this generation we hear little talk by our governing officials about unalienable rights. Rather, the outcry has been for civil rights. Civil rights are "rights" created and granted by human government but unalienable rights are in the nature of things and cannot be endowed by man. Government is not God with authority to grant rights. It is God's minister and man's servant to protect the rights God has given man. Freedom of worship, speech and assembly are rights, not priveleges to be granted or revoked by government institutions.

As long as a nation recognizes that it is God who bestows

human rights, he will protect the liberties of all. If human government endows rights, then we are threatened with the tyranny of the majority, an oligarchy or dictatorship. When God is forsaken, might makes right — whether it be political or military — and the result is the same. No one has the right to be a homosexual, thief or murderer because God's law forbids such practices. We do have the right to worship, freedom to speak (but not blasphemy), to own property and enjoy the fruits of our labor. There is a higher law than the Constitution. Failure to recognize this fact is the road to despotism.

Capitalism Versus Socialism

"Shut up, you capitalist pig," growled a hairy rebel wearing a red beret. He was walking around the crowd selling communist newspapers.

"Young man, I'm glad to see you engaged in a capitalistic enterprise. That's how I got my start as a paper boy. Keep up the work. You may be a corporate executive someday. Many of our nation's wealthiest men started the ladder of success as a lowly paper boy," I mocked.

The crowd laughed and he cursed me as he unsuccessfully tried to sell his propaganda.

While the students will ignore someone this blatant, they have accepted the more subtle brainwashings of their professors against the free enterprise system.

As an undergraduate, I majored in social studies and after graduation taught it in the public schools. Social studies in actuality is a guise to deceive students with socialism. They do not call it socialism because taxpayers would object if they knew their money was being spent to tear down the free enterprise system that made America economically great. Capitalism has provided people with the highest standard of living and with the most freedom any country in the history of the world has known. Not only have Americans benefitted but this country is the breadbasket of the world.

Radical students of the 60s merely attempted to put into

social practice ideas they had learned in the classroom. As a hippie in Morocco, I was amazed that the young men there, without exception, wanted to come to America. I had come to regard Americans as "the imperialists" who were exploiting "the third world." Hearing the eagerness of the Moroccans to leave family and friends for the land of opportunity influenced me to reconsider my attitude about my native land and to return to it.

Many college students are convinced that Jesus was a socialist revolutionary. The liberation theology promoted by the World Council of Churches is nothing but socialism in religious terminology. It is significant that when Jesus began his public life in Israel the nation was under the martial law of Rome. The "human rights" of the Jews were being usurped by the Romans. Yet, Jesus did not advocate a social or political revolution. He advocated a moral regeneration in the hearts of men. He said: "Ye must be born again" (John 3:7). Or, a person must turn from a self-centered life to a God-centered life. His emphasis was on human responsibilities rather than human rights.

There are two methods of social change: regeneration and revolution. The reasonable man chooses regeneration by publishing the Gospel and peacefully attempting to implement the laws of God into his society.

In the parable of the talents (a talent is a sum of money) the Lord did not equally distribute the wealth to his servants (as the socialists advocate) but "gave to every man according to his several ability," not his need. To the one with most ability he gave only one talent. The first two servants put their money with the investors and doubled it. But the third servant buried his talent. Later the Lord returned for an accounting and commended the first two for doubling their money. But the third servant he rebuked as being wicked and slothful for not at least putting the money in the bank and gaining interest. The Lord commanded that the unprofitable servant's talent should be taken and given to the one with the 10 talents. He said: "For unto everyone that hath shall be given, and he shall have abundance: but from him that hath not shall be taken away even that which he hath." In order words take from the have nots (or will nots) and give more to the haves. Finally, he commands the unprofitable servant to be cast into HELL (Matthew 25:14-30).

The foundation of capitalism is private property. God puts his seal of approval on private ownership in the eighth commandment, "Thou shalt not steal" and in the 10th commandment, "Thou shalt not covet (unlawfully desire) thy neighbor's property." Socialists are covetous thieves who want to spend other people's money and rob workers of the fruits of their labor.

Liberation theologians (socialists) like to argue that the early church practiced communism. But the state did not take the Christians' land and houses. They voluntarily sold their possessions and gave the money to the apostles to give to others in need. The difference being the CHURCH, and not the STATE, received and distributed the wealth. This was done voluntarily and not through force or taxation.

Peter reaffirmed the unalienable right of private property to Ananias when Peter said that Ananias was lying to the Holy Spirit about holding back part of the price of his land. Peter asked: "While it remained, was it not thine own? and after it was sold, was it not in thine own power?" (Acts 5:4).

However, this "communism" in the early church is not to be considered the norm for Christians today. First of all there was a particular crisis situation which existed in Jerusalem. Thousands of Jews had been suddenly converted. Many of these from all over the Roman Empire were visiting Jerusalem to celebrate Pentecost and instead of returning to their home countries they stayed in the city to be taught their new faith. There was also great persecution against the church and Christians reasoned that holding things in common would strengthen their position.

Third, Jerusalem was condemned property because Jesus had prophesied the city would be destroyed. Therefore, the Christians needed to get prepared to leave.

The primary question between socialism and capitalism is this: Who or what determines the goods or services that will be produced or provided in a society? The socialist answers "the government made up of an elite group of planners;" the capitalist replies "the free operation of the market."

Capitalism is the more just and equitable system because each time the individual buys or sells on the market he casts his vote for the goods or services that will be produced and provided.

The successful capitalist must sacrifice for the present to gain capital for the future. He must be wise and risk producing a product or providing a service that he believes the public will buy. If he succeeds it is because he is efficiently providing a product or service the public wants.

Economic, political and religious freedom are all tied together. Second only to religious freedom is a man's privilege to enjoy the fruit of his own labor. However, to enjoy this privilege, one must fulfill his responsibility to work. God's Word says: "If any would not work, neither should he eat" (II Thessalonians 3:10).

Socialists accuse the Christians and the conservatives who oppose the welfare state of lacking compassion for the poor. Christians recognize a responsibility to the poor but they feel that any help to the poor must be voluntary if it is to be virtuous. The church should aid the genuinely helpless if family or friends fail in their responsibility. The socialist makes a mistake in assuming that if the state does not do it, it will not get done. The U.S. Constitution established the responsibility of the government to "promote the general welfare," but not to provide it. The general welfare will be advanced by government supporting the freedom to buy and sell at will, without state intervention. (An exception would be if an enterprise is against God's law such as traffic in drugs and pornography). Not only would *laissez-faire* economics eliminate government welfare to the poor but also forbid protecting and subsidizing favored industries.

Capital Punishment

Capital punishment is always a controversial issue on campus. The majority of students and faculty oppose the death penalty. It never ceases to amaze me that the same ones who support murdering babies (abortion) are against the state executing convicted criminals. The babies are innocent; the convicts are wicked.

God's law repeatedly commands capital punishment: "Whoso sheddeth man's blood, by man shall his blood be shed: for in the image of God made he man." (Genesis 9:6).

"He that smiteth a man, so that he die, shall surely be put to death" (Exodus 21:12), the Word also admonishes us.

However, murder is not the only crime that demands the death penalty. Levitical Law provides for the public stoning of anyone that curses his parents, commits adultery, incest, homosexuality or beastiality (including death for the beast) (Leviticus 20).

But the students argue, "Thou shalt not kill."

Murder is unjustified killing. Capital punishment is justice for capital crimes. Actually, the sixth commandment is more accurately translated murder. Most modern translations read "Thou shalt not murder."

Others protest, "But that is the Old Testament."

I remind them that Jesus came not "to destroy the law, or the prophets: I am not come to destroy, but to fulfill" (Matthew 5:17).

Law without sanctions is merely suggestion. If government does away with the penalty of the law then the precept goes with it. Effective law must include both precept and penalty.

Romans 13 teaches that the governing authorities are the ministers of God to execute wrath upon evildoers. The officials do not "bear the sword in vain." It is the responsibility of good government to execute the penalty of God's law. If leaders refuse to execute capital criminals then the government has become wicked and rebellious against God.

To take away the state's power to enforce the law with capital punishment is an attack on the very foundation of the government.

Chief Justice Warren Burger of the U.S. Supreme Court admitted that "a reign of terror" exists on the streets of America because of the crime, violence and murder that go unpunished.

Since established authority is not protecting property from theft and citizens from violent attacks, vigilante groups such as the "Guardian Angels" have formed taking the law into their own hands.

If constitutional government continues to fail in its basic function to protect those who abide by the law and to punish the lawbreakers, it will crumble. A totalitarian regime will replace it which will establish law and order at the expense of the inalienable rights of life, liberty and property.

If God spared not his own Son who was innocent but delivered him up for us all, who do these moral morons on campus think they are to advocate that the state should set aside the death penalty for those guilty of capital crimes? Anyone who professes to be a Christian and opposes capital punishment reveals his disregard not only for God's law but for the voluntary sufferings of Christ on the cross for the sins of mankind.

*The Pharisees took counsel
how they might entangle Jesus
in his talk. — Matthew 22:15*

19

MORE QUESTIONS
AND ANSWERS

As I preach to the students throughout the afternoon I often pause for questions or comments. Occasionally a serious seeker will have a sincere question. However, most of the inquirers are simply trying to trap me in my speech. Even worse, the majority of the questions asked reflect the typical sinner's attempt to justify his rebellion and condemn God.

How Do We Know the Bible
Is the Word of God?

I have done many surveys on university campuses and found that less than 10 percent of the college students have ever read through one of the four Gospels. Despite their ignorance of the Bible, they are constantly trying to discredit it. If they read the whole Bible, they would be amazed at its unity of themes and lack of contradictions. They would find that contrary to what their professors have taught them the Bible is the most logical, reasonable and practical book that has ever been written. But they are living too selfishly to take time for the Book by which they will one day be judged. They will not research the historical, archaeological and scientific evidences for the scriptures. They are willingly ignorant of the hundreds of biblical prophecies that have been and are continuing to be fulfilled.

Most college students are so woefully ignorant of the scriptures that they cannot even ask an intelligent question. One student informed me he was sure the Bible was not the Word of God because "King Charles was a sinner." (I assume he meant King James).

They claim the Bible has been rewritten or translated so many times that it could not possibly be credible. They ignore the way the Hebrews meticulously copied the sacred writings. They never complain about the translations of Plato, Aristotle, Freud or Marx. If the Bible translations are so inaccurate, why do people of all languages share the common faith? The critics strain at a knat and swallow a camel.

A serious truth-seeker can find overwhelming evidence for the Bible in Josh McDowell's *Evidence That Demands a Verdict* or even better, Charles G. Finney's *The Heart of Truth.*"

Why then do most reject the Bible? Because it is antagonistic to their sinful nature. Every page commands holiness. Madly searching for an excuse to live selfishly, the students ignore the evidence and fall for any line an anti-God professor will give them.

The Bible answers any legitimate question a person could ask about the issues of life. The problem is that most do not like the answer.

Did God Create Evil?

The question that has confounded philosophers throughout the ages is how do you reconcile a benevolent God to the existence of evil in the universe? Did God create evil? If God created evil, how can he be benevolent?

It is important in answering this question that we define our terms.

Benevolence is a disposition to do good from a pure motive. God wills to promote the highest well-being of all and to prevent the highest misery of all. All evil is a result of violation of God's law. "Sin (Evil) is the transgression of the law" (I John 3:4).

God created a heavenly being by the name of Lucifer who was perfect in all of his ways until the day evil was found in him. When Lucifer exalted his will over God's will, evil entered the picture. Evil originated not with God but Lucifer. God does not act against his own will or law.

Why then did God create Lucifer with the ability to do evil? God created Lucifer as a moral being with the ability to choose. There is only virtue where there is freedom of choice.

Mother ties Johnny to the chair and tells him not to get into things and make a mess. Johnny does not make a mess but there is no virtue in his behavior because he had no choice in the matter.

Remember God did not create Satan. Satan means adversary. God created Lucifer which means "Son of Morning." Lucifer chose to become God's adversary and lead a third of the angels in rebellion against God. At this point he became known as Satan.

What about Isaiah 45:7? "I form the light, and create darkness: I make peace, and I create evil." Evil here is used in the sense of calamity as other translations make clear. Calamity and disasters are usually the natural consequences of violating God's Moral Law.

Is God Limited?

A trick question I am invariably asked is, "Can God make a rock that he cannot lift?"

This question results from a false notion of God's omnipotence. God is by nature all-powerful. When God created man he chose to limit his power in that he would not usurp man's free will except according to exceptional exercises of his providence. Man is the rock that God has created that he can not lift, unless man is willing to be lifted out of the pit of sin.

"Yea, they turned back and tempted God, and limited the Holy One of Israel" (Psalm 78:41), the Word tells us.

Actually, there are many things God cannot do and be true to his HOLY character. God cannot lie and be the TRUTH. God cannot be JUST and be unjust. God cannot provide another way to him, and Jesus Christ be The WAY.

Who Created God?

Often students ask absurd and ridiculous questions with an air of intelligence. The most absurd question is "Who created God?"

God by definition is the Creator or First Cause. It is stupid to ask who created the Creator or what caused the First Cause. If something or someone created God, then that someone or something would be God. God had no beginning or end. He always has been and always will be. He is the Alpha and Omega. He is the Beginning and End.

What About the Heathen?

Every day someone asks, "What about those that have never heard of Jesus Christ are they damned?"

Indeed, they are damned but it is not because they have not heard the Gospel. They are damned because they have rejected the light they have through nature and through their consciences. Paul declares that all men will be without excuse on Judgment Day because God has made the truth clear and plain to them through his planned and orderly creation (Romans 1:18-20). Futhermore, Paul states that God has written his law on every man's heart or conscience. Each man knows right from wrong within himself (Romans 2:11-16).

Therefore, since all have sinned, all are guilty before God and condemned. The heathen is not lost because he has rejected

Jesus Christ. How can he believe if he has not heard? The heathen is condemned because he has sinned against the light of nature and his conscience.

The cancer patient is not dying because there is no cure for cancer. He is dying because he has the deadly disease. So it is with the heathen. He is dead in his sins because he has intentionally exposed himself to the deadly disease of sin.

A man's guilt is measured according to his knowledge. Since western man has greater knowledge of God through biblical revelation and living Christian examples, his condemnation will be greater than the heathen's. The heathen will rise up on the day of judgment and condemn civilized man who, by wickedness, suppressed the truth.

Should the heathen, as a result of the witness of nature and his conscience, seek for God, he will move heaven and earth to reveal himself. Commonly, God works through missionaries but he is not limited to that means. He has appeared to the heathen in visions and dreams and he can still do it.

Of course, the real reason this question is asked is not because unbelievers care about the heathen; but they want to accuse God of injustice! They want an excuse to continue in their sin.

What's Wrong With Mohammedism, Buddhism, Hinduism and Other Religions?

Jesus said, "Go ye therefore, and teach all nations, baptizing them in the name of the Father and of the Son and of the Holy Ghost."

He did not say go to Japan and teach and baptize in the name of Buddha, or to China in the name of Confucius, or to India in the name of Krishna and later to the Arab nations in the name of Muhammad. He said teach them (all nations) "whatsoever I have commanded you."

Jesus made it clear that he was the only way to salvation: "I am the door of the sheep." He added: "All that came before me are thieves and robbers" and "I am the Way, and the Truth and the Life: no man cometh to the Father but by me."

"I am the true Vine," he said.

"I am the bread of life. Except ye eat the flesh of the Son of man and drink His blood ye have no life in you,'' he added.

"For if you believe not I am He, ye shall die in your sins," he said.

There are an estimated 900 million Moslems in the world. Millions more are Buddhists and Hindus. Students constantly ask "Are all these people wrong?"

Liberal professors and ministers have said the religions of the world are like many rivers flowing into the same ocean or many paths up the same mountain.

The famed Gandhi was quoted as saying, "I'm a Hindu, a Buddhist, a Moslem, a Jew and a Christian."

Many consider this is a profound statement. But once the facts are examined it becomes an obviously stupid remark. The Bible teaches that Jesus is the only way to God and all other religions are false. Note these words: "Neither is there salvation in any other: for there is none other name under heaven given among men, whereby we must be saved" (Acts 4:12).

If any other religion is true, Jesus was a liar and all Christians are deceived. On the other hand if Christianity is true, no other religion can be correct. It is amazing that students respect someone as irrational as Gandhi and the liberal theologians.

"What makes Christianity so special?"

One word: Atonement.

Atonement refers to the governmental substitution of the suffering of Christ for the punishment of sinners. It is a covering of their sins by his suffering.

Nature and conscience have revealed three things to men everywhere:

1. There is one good God (Benevolent Governor of the universe).
2. All have broken God's moral law.
3. God will judge all in the last day.

Men worldwide ask:
1. How do I get rid of my sins?
2. How can I receive forgiveness?
3. How can I escape judgment?

Some try to merit salvation by good works or by terrible sufferings. Throughout history men have sought ways to appease pagan gods and to rid themselves of the guilt of sin. But their consciences bare witness that they are not forgiven or cleansed from sin so they repeat these practices over and over.

Some teach that mere repentance will bring God's forgiveness. Although God desires to show mercy on the repentant sinner, a blanket pardon would not be just because God's law says, "The soul that sinneth shall surely die." Justice must be executed if men are to respect God and his government. If God were to grant a pardon to men on the grounds of repentance alone, he would be virtually repealing his law. Men would not need to fear punishment because they could repent anytime they please and be forgiven.

Justice must be executed if men are to respect God and his government. A distinction needs to be made between retributive and public justice.

Retributive justice is concerned only with the letter of the law by punishing evildoers according to the exact precepts and sanctions of the law.

Public justice considers the spirit of the law and is primarily concerned with promoting and securing the public interests. If God's justice were strictly retributive, then every soul would be damned to hell for eternity since all have sinned. Although public justice also implies the execution of the law's penalties, an exception can be made if something else can be done that will effectively secure the public interests; then, upon the condition of repentance, God can uphold his law, protect the public interest and pardon the lawbreaker.

Jesus Christ, God's Son, suffered and died on Calvary's Cross as a substitute (the atonement) for the penalty of eternal damnation of sinners, thereby making satisfaction to public justice by demonstration to the world that sin will not go unpunished. Furthermore, showing that Jesus is the only way that men can get rid of their sins, receive forgiveness and escape judgment.

Simply quoting the Bible can sometimes be futile when witnessing to someone of another religious background. Instead, a witness can bring forth scriptural principles by appealing to the evidence of nature and conscience to show the serious seeker that his religion is false.

For example, the Moslems believe one of the seven principle attributes of God is "will." They say everything that exists and happens is according to God's perfect will. That would mean if a man is a murderer or rapist it is because God wills it. The Moslem god condemns man for what he cannot help. The conscience of every Moslem tells him this is absurd. Would a Moslem parent punish a child for disobeying a command he could not keep? Of course not. With a little forethought it is easy to show the Moslem that his god is an unreasonable tyrant and not the Benevolet Moral Governor of the universe revealed everywhere in nature.

Are All Jews Going to Hell?

One day on campus I asked a girl, "Are you a Christian?" She replied, "No, I am a Jew."

"Jesus was born a Jew, he came to the Jews first, and all his initial disciples were Jews. One of the greatest Jews who ever lived was the Apostle Paul of the tribe of Benjamin," I said.

Paul wrote, "I am not ashamed of the Gospel of Chist: for it is the power of God unto salvation to everyone — who believeth; to the Jew first, and also to the Greek" (Romans 1:16).

I added, "If you're a Jew that is all the more reason to be a Christian."

Angrily, she replied, "If I were a Christian, I wouldn't be a Jew anymore."

"What is a Jew?" I asked.

She gave the answer I have heard many times from Jewish students, "A Jew is one who doesn't believe in Jesus."

This statement tells me two things. One, most Jews on campus are shamefully ignorant of the history of their fathers, the faith of Abraham and Moses and their own Holy Scriptures. Two, for most of these descendents of Abraham being Jewish is just another excuse to reject the truth of God, remain stiff-necked, uncircumcised at heart and continue in their sins. There are multitudes of people who do not believe in Jesus: Buddhists, Hindus, Moslems and most college students. Certainly this does not make them Jews.

Some students will add, "The Jews are God's chosen people. We don't need Jesus."

They have never heard the conditions that God told the Hebrews they must meet to be his people: "Now therefore, if ye will obey my voice indeed, and keep my covenant then ye shall be a peculiar treasure unto me above all people: for all the earth is mine: and ye shall be unto me a kingdom of priests, and a holy nation. These are the words which thou shall speak unto the children of Israel" (Exodus 19:5, 6).

Most Jews on campus have never read the 613 laws of Moses, much less kept them. Neither have they read that there are great curses placed by God on any Jew that does not keep all his commands, "Cursed be he that confirmeth not all the words of this law to do them. And all the people shall say, Amen" (Deuteronomy 27:26).

There is only one Jew throughout history who has never broken God's law. He is the Lord Jesus Christ.

What about all the rest of the Jews? Is there no hope for them? God forbid! Their own scriptures give them their only hope. ". . . for it is the blood that maketh an atonement for the soul" (Lev. 17:11). Only a blood sacrifice can provide forgiveness of sins. The Hebrew scriptures prove that Jesus of Nazareth became that sacrifice for every Jew who has ever lived (Isaiah 53, Psalm 22).

John the Baptist, a Jew of the tribe of Levi, knew this. That is why the moment he saw Jesus, he said, "Behold the Lamb of

God that takes away the sins of the world." John was speaking to a crowd of Jews who, being familiar with the passover, understood Levi's statement. As a result of John's witness, a number of Jews believed in Jesus as the Messiah and began to follow him (Matthew 1:35-49).

I have said on campus that any Jew who will seriously study the Old Testament (Hebrew scriptures) prophecies of the Messiah must conclude that Jesus of Nazareth fulfilled them. He is indeed the Savior of Israel and the world.

As a result of my preaching some Jews have recognized their failure to keep the law of Moses and their great need for Jesus the Messiah. One was Phil S. at the University of Illinois. Here is the powerful testimony he wrote after his conversion:

> The Lord said to me recently, 'Publicize yourself, and let people know that you are a Christian.' So I am writing this paper to let people know who the Lord Jesus Christ used to convert me from the road of sin that is headed toward hell and certain damnation, to the narrow path of deliverance in belief in Christ.
>
> As a child, years ago, I was taught in the beliefs of Judaism. I was told that the Jews don't believe in Jesus being the Messiah, but never told why. I developed a curiosity about Christianity. I felt that since more than one-half of the country's population were what I considered Christian, I should find out what it was that turned them to Jesus in the first place.
>
> Being from a Jewish home, I didn't have access to a New Testament, so my curiosity about Christianity diminished, and I forgot about it until the Fall of 1978, when I came down to this campus from Chicago as a freshman. By chance I happened to hear brothers Max Lynch and Jed Smock preaching in the Quad.
>
> I listened to them preaching, and to the crowd that was constantly heckling them, and found much amusement in the remarks that the crowd shouted at them. Although I didn't believe in what they were saying, I stayed out there

listening because it kept me from spending the time playing pinball in the Illini Union.

On Ash Wednesday, 1979, I received a Bible from the Gideon people, who were passing them out on every street corner. After a while I started believing in some of the things that Max and Jed were saying out on the Quad; and if I had a question I could ask them for an answer, or I would look for an answer in the Bible.

If I couldn't find the answer that I wanted, I would ask one of my friends, Bob. I discovered that Bob was a Christian last semester, when I walked into his room while he was in the middle of a Bible study with some other believers. After that day, he was willing to help me in my struggle for the truth. He suggested that I read the book of John, and I did getting some powerful meanings out of it.

Summer came, however, and I succumbed to more sin, drunkenness, lust and drugs. Coming down to school again in August, I discovered that my new roommate Jeff was a "born again" person. The presense of the Holy Ghost on his side of the room seemed to rub off on me, as I decided to give up drinking and drugs. My trips through the Quad started again, and I became acquainted with Sister Cindy Lasseter. I started becoming more receptive to the Word of God, and began to ask questions of her. She began to connect the two testaments of the Bible together, by showing me where everything about Jesus was prophesied in the Old Testament. I was still unsure about the validity of Christianity, so I began to pray to God to tell me what was the true path. I reached the point where I thought that I believed, but wasn't ready to make a commitment for Christ. In a further attempt to find the truth, I went to a Bible study on August 28, led by Jed Smock. Near the end of the Bible study Jed started to pray for our souls, and when we joined him in prayer I had a weird experience. I became tense, and felt as though electricity was flowing through my body, not letting me move my joints. I knew that something was going on in my body, but I wasn't sure what it was.

Later that night I decided that I should be born again. I was unsure about how to go about it, so the next day I talked to Cindy on the Quad, and decided to go through with it. So at 8:20 p.m. that night I sat down in the middle of the Quad and prayed for forgiveness, and asked Lord Jesus to come inside me, to guide my ways, and to keep me from straying. Immediately after I got up, a feeling of complete contentment and peace came over me. Later that night I was going to smoke a cigarette, because I knew of nothing in the Bible against smoking. But I heard a voice in my head that said, "Would you rather save some money, then keep the body that I have given you from being destroyed?" This was connected to the fact that I had not wanted to throw away the cigarettes because I thought that that would be a waste of money that I paid for them. I found out that if I wanted Jesus to come inside me, that he didn't want to live in a smoke filled room. Needless to say, I threw away my cigarettes that night, and haven't had one since.

The next night, I was baptized with water in a swimming pool, and today as I write this, I am a new Man.

I can't think of an ending for this paper, for it is not over yet. I am still learning and growing spiritually.

Phil is just one of the many Jews our preaching has influenced. A Jewish girl at Louisiana State University confessed that she hated Christians but she did respect Sister Cindy. Returning to campus a year later we found the girl was converted, had led two Moslems to the Lord Jesus and was involved with a strong Christian group.

Sister Cindy has commented how she will never forget her Friday night visit to the Hillel Center at the University of Wisconsin. To her amazement she discovered that the young rabbi (a guest speaker) did not believe there is a God. He told her this privately, quickly adding that he would pray to God for Jewish people who asked him to. This confused youth said he considered himself a leader of Israel.

The resident Rabbi was older and more conservative. He told Sister Cindy that it was pagan to believe God has a son. Had not he read his own scriptures? "Who hath ascended up into heaven, or descended? Who hath gathered the wind in His fist? Who hath bound waters in a garment? Who hath established all the ends of the earth? What is His name? What is His Son's name, if thou canst tell?" (Proverbs 30:4).

At University of Arizona, Rabbi Morton Levine of the Hillel Foundation was quoted in the newspaper as saying, "We're expecting an upsurge (in Jewish students at Hillel) now that Jed Smock is back. A lot of Jews come here because they don't know how to react."

I have found that many Jews who come to Christ often start by going back to synagogue; when they see the emptiness of modern-day Judaism they usually begin examining the faith of Abraham and Moses as revealed in the scriptures. This points them to the Messiah.

Where Do You Get Your Money?

When students find they cannot discredit my message, they attempt to find fault with me. They accuse me of being in the ministry for financial gain. The students refuse to admit that I am motivated by the love of God, so they frantically search for other motives.

They ask such questions as: "How much money to you make?" "Why do you drive a new automobile?" "Where do you get those $500 three-piece suits?" "Do you pay taxes?" "Just how do you get your money, anyway?"

When God calls a man into a ministry, it is his responsibility to provide the means. The Word says: "God shall supply all your needs according to his riches in glory by Christ Jesus" (Philippians 4:19). God sometimes has unusual ways of doing it.

One year when I was preaching at UCLA, a Jewish rabbi had been questioning me for several days. This man admitted to being a Pharisee. One day he asked me to read Luke 6:30.

I read, "Give to every man that asketh of thee: and of him that taketh away thy goods ask them not again."

The rabbi said, "Do you believe that?"

"Every word of God is true." I answered.

"Well, give me your watch then," he challenged.

I had a nice digital watch that a friend had recently given to me; but nevertheless, I took it off and gave it to the rabbi.

I said, "God is able to give me a better watch."

That evening I was speaking in a local church. Some of the members had been helping me on campus and they told the pastor how I had given away my watch. The pastor said to his congregation, "Let's pray that God gives Brother Smock a new watch and not a $49.95 Timex but a good watch."

Before the prayer a man who had never been in the church before or since raised his hand and said, "I have just the watch for Brother Smock."

The next day he presented me with an expensive Seiko quartz chronograph — the Cadillac of watches!

I went back out to campus and showed the crowd my new watch. The rabbi came on the scene again and said, "Give me that watch."

I answered, "Rabbi, I understand you believe the Old Testament."

That's right," he replied.

"Do you believe the 10 commandments?" I asked.

He answered, "Of course, I am a Jew."

"Rabbi, the 10th commandment says thou shalt not covet. You are coveting my watch. God did not give it to you, but to me."

The laughing crowd sided with me and that silenced the rabbi.

I speak in churches and to Christian organizations which usually give me an offering or honorarium. In addition, there are individuals who have taken an interest in my ministry who make donations. I have never solicited any money on the campuses. Occasionaly a student or professor does make a gift.

One Friday at Louisiana State University, late in the afternoon, a student said, "Brother Jed, I want to give you this $10 bill. I had been planning on going out and getting drunk this afternoon but instead I have stayed here listening to you; and I want you to have the money I saved."

That evening I was speaking to the Chi Alpha Christian organization. That student attended the meeting. After my message he came forward to confess Jesus as his Lord and Savior. That $10 was not the biggest offering I ever received on campus but considering the testimony that resulted it was one of the best.

When the students see that God has blessed me financially, they become envious. They attempt to hide their envy under the cloak of sympathy for the poor: "Why don't you sell your new automobile and give the money to the poor?" This is said, not that they care for the poor, but because they resent my prosperity. It is not so much that they want what I have but they want me to be deprived of it.

The same might be said of my spiritual prosperity. These guilt manipulators envy the purpose of life and peace of mind that the Christian possesses but they do not want to forsake their selfishness and take up their cross in order to experience it. They are not merely content to attempt to discredit me or Christianity. They want to rob every Christian of his purpose and peace by making him feel guilty for his prosperity, which is God's blessing.

I shall not cease from mental strife,
Nor shall my pen sleep in my hand,
Till I have seen God's holy men
Arise and shake our needy land.
              — Leonard Ravenhill

20

WILL YOU?

In over a decade of preaching on the campuses I have ventured body, blood, wealth and honor for the glory of God. It has been a costly battle. My heart is broken over the great dishonor that America's educational system has brought to the God of the Universe.

Foreign students come to this country expecting to find a Christian people; but they soon see that those called by Christ's name are obsessed with all manner of sin and iniquity. The prophecy has come true: "Thou has built thy places (universities) at the head of every way and has made thy beauty (Christian heritage) to be abhorred, and has opened thy feet to everyone (philosophies and vain deceits) that passes by and multiplied thy whoredoms."

How long will his holy name be dragged through the mud? How long will the blood of the Son of God be trampled on? How long will the wicked be allowed to accuse God falsely? I grieve that no one will defend or speak on behalf of God against his enemies. No one will witness on behalf of his benevolent character.

My love for God and for the students has compelled me to spare no sacrifice to defend truth on the campuses. All of my life has been spent close to the university community. I long to see the colleges return to their religious foundation and once again glorify God. Revival for the universities has been my daily prayer for years. My desire is that professors will again encourage their students to a right relationship with God. It has been distressing to me that my own brethren have accused me of lacking love when I stand against sin.

Through it all I have never considered giving up the crusade. There is no place I would rather be, nothing else I would prefer to be doing than proclaiming the Word of God in the center of campus. I would exchange ministries with no man. I anticipate continuing in the work to which God has called me until I draw my last breath.

How could I stop or even slow down when hundreds of thousands of students are rushing madly toward the everlasting torments of hell-fire? The bottomless pit is waiting to swallow them forever. There will be no hope, no escape for the damned soul. The cries of weeping and wailing will endlessly emanate from the swollen tongues and parched lips of the damned. Protruding eyeballs will stare blindly into outer darkness looking but not seeing. The stench of burning, emaciated flesh will cause maggot-infested nostrils to quiver in endless repulsion. Terribly tormented minds which have long since had every honest, pure and lovely thought twisted out of them will tortuously agonize in dispair over their unendurable calamity. Horrifying blasphemy will shriek from the voices of the lost toward an absent God. Dreadful denunciations of hideous fiends who are relentlessly torturing the wretched, and vile-swearing between former companions in wickedness will ring through the chambers of the abyss.

"Wow, woe, WOE is me" the dead will cry. "My punishment is more than I can bear." No hope! No hope! Endless WOE. No deliverance, no alleviation, no solace, no rest, no sleep, no respite! It will become worse and worse as eternity progresses.

Yet God does not want any to be damned but all to come to repentance. Do you think that God takes pleasure in the death of the sinful? No! God is broken-hearted because of whorish hearts and lecherous eyes that go a-whoring after idols. Man's sins have brought unspeakable disappointment and grief to our Heavenly Father. He longs to save and rejoice over his most noble creation and looks forward to happy fellowship throughout eternity. The Lord is slow to execute judgment for he is gracious, kind and merciful. He is calling to you, "How long, you simple ones, will you love simplicity? and the scorners delight in their scorning, and fools hate knowledge? Turn you at my reproof: behold, I will pour out my spirit unto you, I will make known my words unto you."

SINNER, do not mistake God's forbearance for weakness. Not a day passes when God is not angry with the wickedness on the campuses and the hypocrisy in the churches. "For the Lord, whose name is Jealous, is a jealous God." He is anxious for your loyalty and devotion. All shall stand before the consuming fire of his judgments. I have preached unto you, but you have laughed and mocked. I have told you the truth, but you have chosen to believe a lie. Therefore the Lord is furious; the Lord will take vengeance on his adversaries and store up wrath for his enemies. Can anyone stand before his indignation? Can you live in the fierceness of his anger?

Sinner, what charge do you have against your Creator? How has he ever wronged you? It is only just and reasonable that you should obey him. What excuse do you have for dishonoring him? He has nourished and brought you up from childhood? Why have you rebelled against him? Even your pets — your dogs and your cats — know their owner and appreciate your care for them, but do you not care for your Maker? No matter how much he does for you, you are not concerned. What more could he do for you than he has already done? He causes the sun to rise not only on the good but the evil. He waters the crops of not only the just but the unjust as well. He has provided the fruit on the tree, your vegetables in the ground, the beasts in your fields for meat. Not only has he supplied so abundantly but with such great beauty. But you have been so blinded by your selfishness that you have the audacity to even question his existence! When you have provoked the Holy One to the point that he must punish you, then you curse him and rebel even more.

God's plan for man was to develop such a character in him as to make him like unto his Creator. He intended man to be a co-worker with him in ordering his perfect creation. But man has spurned God's purpose and made it necessary for him to bring about major alternations in his program. It has been grievous for God to watch man choose to be an outlaw when he was designed to be a privileged son to honor him.

Man's sin has brought great dishonor and disgrace and shame to the Almighty who planned so carefully to bring about man's happiness. Oh, the anguish, the heartache, the agony that our Heavenly Father experiences over his rebellious children. Oh, people, people, can you continue to hurt his tender heart? Oh, he has done all that he can justly do to save your wretched souls and soften your rebellious hearts. He has sent his only begotten Son, the Lord Jesus Christ, who was a man of sorrows, experiencing a broken heart because man despised and rejected him. Oh, sinner, there is nothing more, no greater price that can be paid than a man laying down his life for you. Yet you still hold him in disdain and contempt. His last words from Calvary's Cross ring out through the ages on behalf of man, "Father, forgive them for they know not what they do!"

Consider your ways, sinner. "What does it profit a man to gain the whole world and lose his soul? What have you given in exchange for your soul?" It is insane and utter folly for you to continue traveling on the wide side to destruction. There will be no sex, booze, drugs or rock 'n roll in HELL. It is nonsensical to think you will be partying with your "friends" in the infernal regions. Your fame, your fortune, your career will profit you nothing in the abobe of the damned. The fleeting pleasures of this world are but a blink of the eye compared to the timelessness of eternity in the LAKE OF FIRE. A moment there will burn out all the enjoyments of sin in this present life. Stop and think, sinner! Do not play the fool any longer. JUDGMENT DAY IS AT HAND. TURN OR BURN! REPENT OR PERISH! SALVATION OR DAMNATION! HEAVEN OR HELL! JESUS OR THE DEVIL! It is your choice. The Spirit of God will not always strive with man!

CHRISTIAN STUDENT groups, you profess the fundamentals of the faith. You claim to believe in hell. But, do you really? If you really believed, you would sound the alarm. Friendship evangelism, the four spiritual laws, book tables and Bible studies fall woefully short. The night is far spent. Awake unto righteousness. Put away your sin. Warn the wicked. Reprove. Rebuke. Exhort. Forsake your compromising religion, stand up against the godless professors and rise against the wickedness that surrounds you.

PASTORS, most of you have ignored the thousands of students in your community. You sermonize about the last days but your actions betray you by saying to the world there is plenty of time. You give your dispensational sermons on prophecy but you do not take seriously your own words. "But if the watchman see the sword come, (whatever your eschatology is, surely you see judgment is inevitable!) and blow not the trumpet, and the people be not warned; if the sword come, and take any person from among them, he is taken away in his iniquity; but his blood will I require at the watchman's hand."

Many of the people even in your "evangelical" or "full gospel" churches are headed for HELL. You are comforting them in their sins and giving them a false assurance of their salvation. Their blood will be on your hands. REPENT PASTORS! Declare the whole counsel of God. God is sick and tired of your religion of renewal without REVIVAL, love without LAW, deliverance without REPENTANCE, gifts without FRUITS, mercy without JUSTICE, blessings without SUFFERINGS, CHRISTIANITY without COMMITMENT. FAITH without WORKS is dead! Your churches are so far removed from New Testament Christianity it is pitiful. The cults are inspiring people more than you are. "Remember therefore from whence thou are fallen, and repent, and do the first works; or else I will come unto thee quickly, and will remove thy candlestick out of his place, except thou REPENT."

UNGODLY PROFESSOR, you speak great swelling words of vanity, flippantly saying, "There is no God." But your heads are empty. You promise students intellectual freedom, free love, free thinking, but are yourselves bound hand and foot to sin. For a man is a slave of whatever masters him. You are controlled by your own lies and corruptions. Professing yourselves to be wise, you have become the dupes of Darwinism, Freudianism and Marxism. Masters of deceit, servants of Satan, the blackest of darkness is reserved for you forever. You manipulate the unstudied minds of blank-headed youth to smother any spark of faith in their consciousness. It would be better for a millstone to be hanged about your neck, and that you be drowned in the depths of the sea, than for you to continue to mislead your pupils.

COLLEGE DEAN, you condone infidels in the lecturn but some of you have opposed preachers on campus. You have shirked your responsibility to discipline the youth under your charge. Yet at times you have arrested preachers who have tried to resist the floodtide of immorality. Dean, if you are considering stopping the preachers, give attention to the advice of an ancient educator, and the Pharisee, Dr. Gamaliel, "Refrain from these men, and let them alone: for if their counsel or work be of men, it will come to nought: But if it be of God, ye cannot overthrow it; lest haply ye be found even to fight against God."

LAYMEN, where is your strength? Why are you so soft? You have violated the Holy Covenant that God has made with his people. You plead, "Jesus died for my sins," as you continue to sin, and refuse to obey his commandments. You have forsaken the faith of your fathers for a testament without law. Daniel the prophet warned, "Such as do wickedly against the covenant shall be corrupted by flatteries." You have appointed unto yourselves ministers who pander to your sins. Know the God of the sacred scriptures who commands, "Be ye Holy; for I am Holy." You enter the sanctuary and plead, "Lord, meet my needs." If you really knew your God you would stand firm, take action against your own sins and save yourselves from this crooked, perverse generation. Find an altar and cry out, "Lord, what can I do for you?" The Bible says: "Even as the Son of man came not to be ministered unto, but to minister, and to give his life as a ransom from many."

Laymen, are you greater than your Lord? As the Father sent Jesus, he has sent us. Put on the whole armour of God. You have forgotten the breastplate of righteousness. Get activated. When you become righteous and holy, you will be bold and courageous. Rise up against evil, take the shield of faith and draw the sword of the Spirit. Go forth into battle, following the Captain of your Salvation, and destroy the works of the devil.

It was necessary for me to write this book "and exhort you that you should earnestly contend for the faith which was once delivered unto the saints." Saint Daniel challenged us, "The people that know their God shall be strong and do exploits!" ONWARD CHRISTIAN SOLDIERS!

When Paul was under arrest and giving his defense before King Agrippa, Governor Festus accused him of being mad. Many times I have been accused of being crazy but I reply as Paul, "I am not mad, but speak forth the words of truth and soberness." My ministry should not be considered unusual, but normal Christianity.

CHURCH, if a revival spirit truly prevailed, every state university would have a regular campus preacher. A voice of repentance would be crying out daily in the streets from each city across the nation. There would be no parade, festival, demonstration or rock concert without a number of Christians witnessing and some preaching. Abortion clinics and pornography stores would be systematically and relentlessly picketed. P.T.A., school boards and city councils would have diligent Christian watchmen attending meetings. Nursing homes, jails, orphanages would not want for unofficial chaplains. Clergyman would be as active in city and state affairs as lawyers are. If the evangelical churches were as truly committed and consecrated to the cause of Christ as they claim, indeed this would be the typical scene across America today. Imagine the impact on this country if every preacher would come out of his hole tomorrow and find a public forum to declare his faith. "Is there not a cause?"

Although Festus thought Paul to be out of his mind, Agrippa was impressed with Paul's testimony and said, "Paul, almost thou persuadest me to be a Christian."

And Paul answered, "I would to God, that not only thou, but also all that hear me this day, were both almost, and altogether such as I am, except these bonds."

Sinner, we have no evidence that Agrippa was ever converted, even though he had been deeply moved by Paul's message. Obviously, you have been affected by my ministry or you would not have read this far. What are you going to do, lightly pass me off as a raving manic like Festus? Or refuse to pay the price of salvation like Agrippa? Or recognize that you have lived selfishly all of your life, forsake your sins and follow Christ, even as Paul?

BELIEVER, I would that all of you that have heard Paul and have read my book would be as he was and I am — except for being arrested. What kind of a Christian was Paul? He was the only kind of Christian — a minister and a witness. He was a true disciple who was able to say, "Follow me even as I follow Christ." He was a fighter for the cause and a soldier of the Cross. He was blameless. He was a man with a vision who was able to conclude toward the end of his days, "Whereupon, O King Agrippa, I was not disobedient unto the heavenly vision, but have showed men everywhere that they should repent and turn to God, and do works meet for repentance."

God has given me a vision to reach the campuses with the Gospel and bring revival to the churches. With the help of God I continued unto this day on the college campuses and in the churches proclaiming the truth that Jesus Christ suffered and died and rose again the third day to save us from our sins. I pray that on Resurrection Day I will be able to say, "King Jesus, I was not disobedient unto my heavenly vision."

Dear reader, my prayer for you is that this book has increased your vision and understanding of what it means to be a Christian; that you will walk in the brighter light that these words have shined into your heart. Rise up!

The End

THE CAMPUS MINISTRY

Fill out the following and send to:
Jed Smock
The Campus Ministry
173 Woodland Avenue
Lexington, KY 40502
(606) 254-6003

☐ Please send me Jed Smock's Newsletter *The Campus Ministry.*

☐ Please send me a list of Jed Smock's tapes.

☐ I want to be saved from my sins and rise up against evil.

☐ I am enclosing an offering of $_____
for Jed Smock and The Campus Ministry.

☐ I would like for Jed Smock to preach in my church or to my organization.

NAME _____

ADDRESS _____

CITY _____

STATE _____ ZIP _____

MORE FAITH-BUILDING BOOKS
FROM HUNTINGTON HOUSE

The Agony of Deception, by Ron Rigsbee. This is the story of a young man who through surgery became a woman and now, through the grace of God, is a man again. Share this heart-warming story of a young man as he struggles through the deception of an altered lifestyle only to find hope and deliverance in the Grace of God.

America Betrayed, by Marlin Maddoux. This book presents stunning facts on how the people of the United States have been brainwashed. This hard-hitting new book exposes the forces in our country which seek to destroy the family, the schools and our values. Maddoux is a well-known radio journalist and host of "Point of View."

Backward Masking Unmasked — Backward Satanic Messages of Rock and Roll Exposed, by Jacob Aranza. Are rock and roll stars using the technique of backward masking to implant their own religious and moral values into the minds of young people? Are these messages satanic, drug-related and filled with sexual immorality? Jacob Aranza answers these and other questions.

Close Calls, by Don Garlits. Many times "Big Daddy" Don Garlits has escaped death — both on and off the drag racing track. This is the story of drag racing's most famous and popular driver in history. Share his trials and triumphs and the Miracle of God's Grace in his heart.

The Divine Connection, by Dr. Donald Whitaker. This is a Christian Guide to Life Extension. It specifies biblical principles for how to feel better and live longer.

Globalism: America's Demise, by William Bowen, Jr. A national bestseller, this book warns us about the globalists — some of the most powerful people on earth — and their plans to totally eliminate God, the family and the United States as we know it today. Globalism is the vehicle the humanists are using to implement their secular humanistic philosophy to bring about their one-world government.

God's Timetable for the 1980's, by Dr. David Webber. This book presents the end-time scenario as revealed in God's Word and carefully explained by Dr. Webber, the Radio Pastor of the highly acclaimed Southwest Radio Church. This timely book deals with a wide spectrum of subjects including the dangers of the New Age Movement, end-time weather changes, robots and biocomputers in prophecy.

The Hidden Dangers of the Rainbow, by Constance Cumbey. This #1 National Bestseller was the first book to fully expose the New Age Movement. The Movement's goal is to set up a one-world order under the leadership of a false messiah.

Murdered Heiress ... Living Witness, by Dr. Petti Wagner. This is the story of Dr. Petti Wagner — heiress to a large fortune — who was kidnapped and murdered for her wealth, yet through a miracle of God lives today.

A Reasonable Reason to Wait, by Jacob Aranza. God speaks specifically about premarital sex, according to Aranza. The Bible also provides a healing message for those who have already been sexually involved before marriage.

Rest From the Quest, by Elissa Lindsey McClain. This is the candid account of a former New Ager who spent the first 29 years of her life in the New Age Movement, the occult and Eastern Mysticism. This is an incredible inside look at what really goes on in the New Age Movement.

Take Him to the Streets, by Jonathan Gainsbrugh. Well-known author David Wilkerson says this book is "...immensely helpful ..." and "...should be read ..." by all Christians who yearn to win lost people, particularly through street ministry. Effective ministry techniques are detailed in this how-to book of street preaching. The vast, counter-culture flood of teenage drug abuse, alcoholism and immorality have reached into even the smallest towns and cities of America. Carefully read and applied, this book will help you reach these people and others as you *Take Him to the Streets*.

The Twisted Cross, by Joseph Carr. One of the most important works of our decade, **The Twisted Cross** clearly documents the occult and demonic influence on Adolph Hitler and the Third Reich which led to the holocaust killing of more than six million Jews.

Yes, send me the following books:

_____ copy (copies) of **The Agony Of Deception** @ $6.95   = _____
_____ copy (copies) of **America Betrayed** @ $5.95   = _____
_____ copy (copies) of **Backward Masking Unmasked** @ $4.95   = _____
_____ copy (copies) of **Backward Masking Unmasked Cassette Tape** @ $5.95   = _____
_____ copy (copies) of **Close Calls** @ $6.95   = _____
_____ copy (copies) of **The Divine Connection** @ $4.95   = _____
_____ copy (copies) of **Globalism: America's Demise** @ $6.95   = _____
_____ copy (copies) of **God's Timetable For The 1980's** @ $5.95   = _____
_____ copy (copies) of **The Hidden Dangers Of The Rainbow** @ $5.95   = _____
_____ copy (copies) of **Murdered Heiress Living Witness** @ $5.95   = _____
_____ copy (copies) of **A Reasonable Reason To Wait** @ $4.95   = _____
_____ copy (copies) of **Rest From The Quest** @ $5.95   = _____
_____ copy (copies) of **Take Him To The Streets** @ $6.95   = _____
_____ copy (copies) of **The Twisted Cross** @ $7.95   = _____
_____ copy (copies) of **Who Will Rise UP?** @ $5.95   = _____

At bookstores everywhere or order direct from: Huntington House, Inc., P.O. Box 53788, Lafayette, LA 70505.

Send check/money order or for faster service VISA/Mastercard orders call toll-free 1-800-572-8213. Add: Freight and handling, $1.00 for the first book ordered. 50¢ for each additional book.

Enclosed is $ _____ including Postage.

Name _____

Address _____

City _____ State and Zip _____